Student Book

American Headway 3B

Liz and John Soars

OXFORD

UNIVERSITY PRESS

OXFORD
UNIVERSITY PRESS

198 Madison Avenue
New York, NY 10016 USA

Great Clarendon Street
Oxford OX2 6DP England

Oxford New York
Auckland Bangkok Buenos Aires Cape Town
Chennai Dar es Salaam Delhi Hong Kong Istanbul
Karachi Kolkata Kuala Lumpur Madrid Melbourne
Mexico City Mumbai Nairobi São Paulo Shanghai
Taipei Tokyo Toronto

OXFORD is a trademark of Oxford University Press.

American Headway Student Book 3B:
Editorial Manager: Nancy Leonhardt
Managing Editor: Jeff Krum
Senior Production Editor: Joseph McGasko
Associate Production Editor: Nova Ren Suma
Art Director: Lynn Luchetti
Designer: Claudia Carlson
Page Composition: Shelley Himmelstein
Senior Art Buyer/Picture Researcher: Jodi Waxman
Art Buyer: Elizabeth Blomster
Production Manager: Shanta Persaud
Production Coordinator: Eve Wong

Printing (last digit): 10 9 8 7 6 5 4 3 2

Printed in China.

Acknowledgments

Cover concept: Rowie Christopher
Cover design: Rowie Christopher and Silver Editions

Illustrations by:
Carlos Castellanos; Jim DeLapine; Florentina/Piranha Represents;
Roger Penwill

Handwriting and realia by: Claudia Carlson; Karen Minot

Location and studio photography by: Dennis Kitchen Studio;
Jodi Waxman/OUP

*The publishers would like to thank the following for their permission to
reproduce photographs:*
AFP/Corbis, Alaska Stock, Tony Anderson/Getty Images, Archive Photos,
Scott Barrow Inc./International Stock, Bettmann/Corbis, Harrod Blank/
www.artcaragency.com, James Blank/Index Stock, Maryelizabeth Blomster,
Matthew Borkoski/Index Stock, Michael Brennan/Corbis, Claudia Carlson/
OUP, Myrleen Cate/Index Stock, Jason Childs/FPG, Pedro Coll/AgeFotostock,
Corbis, Pablo Corral/Corbis, Mitch Diamond/Index Stock, George B. Diebold/
The Stockmarket, Robert Discalfani/Photonica, Steve Dunwell Photography
Inc/Index Stock, James Fly/Index Stock, Deborah Gilbert/The Image Bank,
Mark Giolas/Index Stock, Michael Goldman/FPG, Peter Gridley/Getty Images,
Tom Grill/AgeFotostock, Northrop Grumman/Index Stock, Jan Halaska/Index
Stock, Robert Harding Picture Library, John Henley/The Stockmarket, Robert
Holmes/Corbis, Hulton Archive/Getty Images, Richard Hutchings/Corbis,
Tomoko Inanami/Photonica, Andrew Itkoff, Dewitt Jones/Corbis, Bill Keefrey/
Index Stock, Michael Keller/The Stockmarket, Bob Krist/Corbis, Bill Lai/
Index Stock, Lightscapes Inc./The Stockmarket, Ryan McVay/Getty Images,
Juan G. Montanes/AgeFotostock, J. P. NACIVET/Getty Images, Photodisc,
photolibrary.com/Index Stock, Phyllis Picardi/International Stock, Roger
Ressmeyer/Corbis, Reuters, Reuters New Media Inc./Corbis, Jon Riley/Index
Stock, Chris M. Rogers/Getty Images, L. Smith/Harstock, Paul A. Souders/
Corbis, Lynn Stone/Index Stock, Keren Su/Index Stock, Superstock, Ken
Usami/Photodisc, Kennan Ward/Corbis, Jodi Waxman/OUP, Alan Wycheck/
Harstock, Jeff Zaruba/The Stockmarket, ZEFA FAST FORWARD/Photonica

Special thanks to: Mike Buttinger; Stan Czyzk at the National Weather Service;
Andrea Levitt; Jeff Perkins; Dennis Woodruff

The publishers would also like to thank the following for their help:
p. 62 "Who Wants to Be a Millionaire?" by Cole Porter. ©1956 Warner
Chappell Music. Used by permission.
p. 65 Amnesty International logo and text Copyright ©Amnesty International.
Used by permission.
World Wildlife Fund logo and text ©World Wildlife Fund. Used by
permission.
Save the Children logo and text ©Save the Children. Used by
permission.
p. 95 "Funeral Blues" copyright 1940 and renewed 1968 by W.H. Auden, from
W.H. Auden: The Collected Poems by W.H. Auden. Used by permission
of Random House, Inc.
p. 96 "My Way" by Paul Anka, Jacques Revaux, Claude Francois, Giles
Thibault. ©1969. Used by permission.

Contents

SCOPE AND SEQUENCE

7 The world of work

Present Perfect active and passive · Phrasal verbs · Leaving a phone message

▶ TEST YOUR GRAMMAR

1 Answer these questions about yourself.

What do you do?

PRESS

1. What do you do?
2. How long have you had your current job?
3. What did you do before that?
4. Which foreign countries have you been to?
5. When and why did you go there?

2 Ask and answer the questions in pairs. Tell the rest of the class about your partner.
Eun-mi is a student.
She's been at Seoul National University for ...
She's been to ...

3 What tenses are used in the questions?

THE JOB INTERVIEW
Present Perfect

1 Read the job advertisement. Do you have any of the qualifications?

BUSINESS JOURNALIST

WORLDWATCH AMERICAS

This international business magazine, with one million readers worldwide, is seeking a journalist, based in Santiago, Chile, to cover business news in Latin America.

Requirements:

- A bachelor's degree in journalism
- At least two years' experience in business journalism
- Fluent in Spanish and English. If possible, have some knowledge of Portuguese
- Excellent communication skills
- International travel experience is a plus

We offer a good salary, full benefits, and paid vacation.

Please send a resume to:

George Butler
WORLDWATCH AMERICAS
7950 Merritts Avenue
Overland Park, IL 51551

2 **T 7.1** Listen to Heather Mann being interviewed by George Butler. Do you think she will get the job? Why or why not?

3 Read the first part of Heather's interview. Complete the sentences with *do, did,* or *have.*

G Who ____*do*____ you work for now, Heather?

H I work for Intertec Publishing. We publish international business magazines.

G I see. And how long _____ you worked there?

H I _____ worked there for five years. Yes, exactly five years.

G And how long _____ you been in charge of East Asia publications?

H For two years.

G And what _____ you do before you were at Intertec?

H I worked as an interpreter for the United Nations.

T 7.1 Listen and check.

GRAMMAR SPOT

1 Does Heather still work for Intertec?
Does she still work for the UN?

2 Heather says:
   I **work** for Intertec Publishing.
   I've **worked** there for five years.
   I **worked** as an interpreter in Geneva.

What are the different tenses?
Why are they used?

▶▶ **Grammar Reference 7.1 and 7.2 p. 145**

4 Read and complete the second part of the interview with *did, was,* or *have.*

G As you know, this job is based in Santiago, Chile. __**Have**__ you ever lived abroad before?

H Oh, yes. Yes, I _____ .

G And when _____ you live abroad?

H Well, in fact, I _____ born in Colombia and I lived there until I was 11. Also, I lived in Geneva for one year when I _____ working for the UN.

G That's interesting. _____ you traveled much?

H Oh, yes. I _____ traveled to most countries in South America and many countries in Europe. I _____ also been to Japan a few times.

G Interesting. Why _____ you go to Japan?

H It _____ for my job. I went there to interview some Japanese business leaders.

T 7.2 Listen and check.

PRACTICE

Biographies

1 Here are some more events from Heather Mann's life. Match a line in **A** with a time expression in **B**.

A	B
1. She was born	for the last five years.
2. She went to school in Bogota	in Colombia in 1973.
3. She studied business and journalism	from 1978 to 1984.
4. She worked in Geneva	at Boston University.
5. She's been to Japan	since she was in Geneva.
6. She's worked for Intertec	yet.
7. She hasn't lived abroad	a few times.
8. She hasn't gotten a job at Worldwatch Americas	for a year before she worked for Intertec.

T 7.3 Listen and check.

2 Make a similar chart for your own life. Ask your partner to match the events and the times to tell the story of your life.

> **WRITING:** Writing a cover letter
> ▶▶ Go to page 116

Talking about you

3 Complete the sentences about you.
1. I haven't learned to … yet. **I haven't learned to swim yet.**
2. I've been at this school since …
3. I've known my best friend for …
4. I've never …
5. My mother/father has never …
6. I started … ago.
7. I've lived in … since …
8. I went to … when I was a child.

Have you ever … ?

4 These verbs are all irregular. What is the Past Simple and Past Participle?

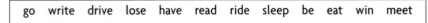

go write drive lose have read ride sleep be eat win meet

5 Work with a partner. Choose from the list below and have conversations.
A Have you ever been to California?
B Yes, I have. / No, I haven't. I've never been there.
A When did you go there?
B Two years ago. I went there on vacation with my family.

- be/to California?
- drive/a truck?
- be/on TV?
- win/an award?
- meet/anyone famous?
- have/an operation?
- have/a serious accident?
- ride/a motorcycle?
- read/a book in English?

Tell the class about your partner.

IT'S IN THE NEWS
Present Perfect active and passive

1 Read the newspaper headlines on page 53. Check any new words.

2 **T 7.4** Read and listen to the TV news headlines of the same stories. Fill in the blanks with the words you hear.

Here are today's news headlines.

1. Convicted murderer Dwayne Locke <u>**has escaped**</u> from the Greenville Correctional Facility in Texas.

2. Two Spanish novelists _____ the Nobel Prize in literature.

3. Hurricane Jeffrey _____ the Caribbean, causing widespread damage in Puerto Rico.

4. Two thousand hotel workers in Anaheim, California _____ due to a slowdown in tourism.

5. Desmond Lewis _____ in the fifth round of his heavyweight championship fight in Las Vegas.

> ### GRAMMAR SPOT
>
> **1** Which of these questions can you answer? Which can't you answer? Why?
>
> Who has escaped from jail?
> Who has given the novelists the Nobel Prize?
> What has hit the Caribbean?
> Who has laid off the hotel workers?
> Who knocked out Desmond Lewis?
>
> **2** Which sentences in Exercise 2 are active? Which are passive?
>
> ▶▶ **Grammar Reference 7.2 p. 145**

NOVELISTS AWARDED NOBEL PRIZE

Hurricane Hits Caribbean

Lewis Knocked Out in 5th Round

Dangerous Prisoner Escapes

HOTEL WORKERS LAID OFF

PRACTICE

Writing news stories

1 Here are some more headlines from newspapers. Make them into TV news headlines. Use the Present Perfect tense.

1. Dangerous Prisoner Recaptured
   The murderer Dwayne Locke has been recaptured by city police.
2. Cruise Ship Sinks Near Florida
   A Sunny Vacations cruise ship has sunk off the coast of Florida, near Miami.
3. Famous Movie Star Leaves $3 Million to Her Pet Cat
4. Priceless Painting Stolen from New York Art Museum
5. Typhoon Kills 20, Leaves 13,000 Homeless
6. 18-Year-Old College Student Elected Mayor
7. Senator Forced to Resign
8. Runner Fails Drug Test

T 7.5 Listen and compare your answers.

2 What's in the news today? What national or international stories do you know?

Discussing grammar

3 Work with a partner and decide which is the correct verb form.
   1. The president *has resigned* / *has been resigned* and a new president *has elected* / *has been elected*.
   2. His resignation *announced* / *was announced* yesterday on television.
   3. "Where *did you go* / *have you gone* on your last vacation?" "To Peru. It was fabulous."
   4. "*Did* John ever *go* / *Has* John ever *been* to Paris?" "Oh, yes. Five times."
   5. The plane *took off* / *has taken off* a few minutes ago.
   6. A huge snowstorm *has hit* / *has been hit* Toronto, where over 50 cm of snow *fell* / *has fallen* in one hour. Residents *have advised* / *have been advised* to stay home.

READING AND SPEAKING
Dream jobs

1 What is your dream job? Close your eyes and think about it. Then answer these questions.

  1. Does the job require a lot of training or experience?
  2. Is it well-paid?
  3. Does it involve working with other people?
  4. Is it indoors or outdoors?
  5. Do you need to be physically strong to do it?
  6. Is it dangerous?
  7. Does it involve travel?

Work with a partner. Ask and answer the questions to guess each other's dream jobs.

2 Here are the stories of three people who believe they have found their dream job.

  Divide into three groups.

  Group A Read about Stanley Karras, the hurricane hunter.

  Group B Read about Linda Spelman, the trapeze artist.

  Group C Read about Michael Doyle, the cowboy in the sky.

  Answer the questions in Exercise 1 about your person.

What do you think?

3 Find a partner from the other two groups and compare information.
  • Which of the jobs do you find most interesting?
  • Would you like to do any of them?

4 Read the other two articles quickly. Answer the questions.
  1. Who <u>gets along well</u> with coworkers?
  2. Who <u>took up</u> gymnastics?
  3. Who hasn't <u>come up with</u> an experiment for space yet?
  4. Whose job <u>was handed down</u> from father to son?
  5. Who is <u>cut off from</u> his/her family?
  6. Who finds it exciting <u>to end up</u> in different cities and countries?
  7. Who wants to <u>carry on</u> working until at least 50?
  8. Who often <u>takes off</u> at a moment's notice?
  9. Who <u>came across</u> an ad?

Language work

The <u>underlined</u> words in Exercise 4 are all phrasal verbs. Match them with a verb or expression from the box below.

start doing (a hobby)	separated
leave the ground and fly	pass down
find yourself somewhere unexpectedly	devise/think of
have a good relationship with	find by chance
continue	

THE HURRICANE HUNTER
"There's no such thing as an average day in my job!"

STANLEY KARRAS works as a meteorologist in Tampa, Florida. It's his job to follow hurricanes by plane and provide information about them to scientists.

How did you get the job? I was working for the National Weather Service in Michigan in the fall of 1995, and I saw a movie with my family called *Storm Chasers*. It was about hurricane hunters and I thought, "Wow, that's an interesting job!" As it happened, two months later I came across an ad for a meteorologist to work with the same people who had made the movie. I applied, was interviewed, and started work here in Tampa in May 1996.

What do you like most about it? I love the travel. I've been all over the world chasing hurricanes. It's exciting to end up in different cities and different countries day after day. If you're a meteorologist, you have to love flying. I also love working with top scientists. I've learned so much from them. For me, it's like a classroom in the sky.

What's an average day like? There's no such thing as an average day in my job! It all depends on the weather, and things are constantly changing. We often take off at a moment's notice to chase storms. I'm the one who decides whether we fly low through a storm. I don't want to take us into a hurricane that could be too strong for us.

Have you made any sacrifices to do this job? Yes, one big one. I'm away from my family. They all live in Pennsylvania. My wife's with me, of course, but her family comes from the Midwest, so we're pretty cut off from them.

What would you like to do next? I'd like to join a space program and be the first meteorologist in space, but I haven't come up with an experiment to do in space yet. There aren't any hurricanes!

What advice would you give to someone who wanted to do your job? Study math and science and get a degree in meteorology. I've taken the hurricane hunter path, but you could be a weather forecaster or do research. It's a fascinating subject and the pay's pretty good.

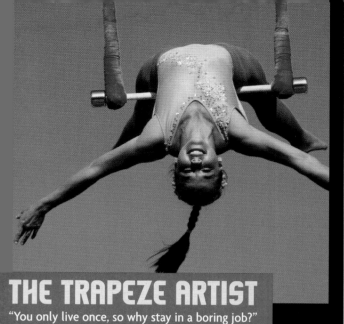

THE TRAPEZE ARTIST

"You only live once, so why stay in a boring job?"

LINDA SPELMAN was a lawyer who found a new career in a circus. She now works as a trapeze artist, traveling with circuses throughout Canada, Europe, and East Asia.

How did you get the job? That's quite a long story. My father's a lawyer, so I thought I'd become one, too. Law school was really, really hard, so I took up gymnastics in the evenings to help me relax. When I finally passed my exams, I thought, "I need a break. I want to travel and learn a language." I'd heard of the Ecole Nationale du Cirque in Montreal, so I thought, "I'll join the circus." I went to Canada and took a trapeze class and, amazingly, I was good at it.

What do you like most about it? The excitement and the travel. I always wanted to travel and learn languages and I've done all of that. Also, I get along really well with circus people. They're all nationalities. I've learned so much about life from them.

What's an average day like? Everyone has to help in the circus, so you begin the day in a new town handing out flyers. In the afternoon, you work in the box office and rehearse. Then you do the act in the evening. At the end of a week, I'm so tired I spend a day in bed. Last month I twisted my shoulder and couldn't work for a week.

Have you made any sacrifices to do this job? No, I haven't, not really. I quit doing something that I hated and I'm doing something that I love. I do miss my family sometimes, but that's all. And of course I earn a lot less than a lawyer.

What would you like to do next? I'm 34 now. I'd like to carry on doing this until I'm at least 50. There are Russian trapeze artists still going strong in their fifties.

What advice would you give to someone who wanted to do your job? You need to be in good shape and strong and have a good head for heights. But generally, I'd say to anyone with a dream, "Go for it! You only live once, so why stay in a boring job?"

THE COWBOY IN THE SKY

"Many of today's ironworkers are descendants of the men who built New York's first skyscrapers."

MICHAEL DOYLE is an ironworker in New York City. He's one of 100 or so ironworkers currently erecting the steel frame of a new 40-story building in Times Square. These ironworkers are known as "cowboys in the sky."

How did you get the job? Ironwork is a trade that is still handed down from father to son. Many of today's ironworkers are descendants of the men who built New York's first skyscrapers. My great-grandfather came over from Ireland in 1930 to work on the construction of the Empire State Building. My father and grandfather were also ironworkers.

What do you like most about it? To me, ironworkers are the kings of construction. We make the skeleton that the other workers build on. We have real pride in our work—you look at the New York skyline and think "I helped build that." Also, we work hard, we play hard. We get along well together. We ironworkers depend on each other for our lives. Oh, and the pay is good!

What's an average day like? You never stop in this job. Eight hours a day, from seven in the morning until three in the afternoon. You're moving all the time. The crane lifts the iron girders and you have to move them into place. There's always danger. It's a fact of life for us.

Have you made any sacrifices to do this job? Yes, one big one—physical health. The wear and tear to the body is enormous. I've fallen three times. My father fell two stories, lost a finger, and broke his ankles.

What would you like to do next? I'd like to work on something real important like my great-grandfather did. Or like my father did, who helped build the World Trade Center. It's weird—he helped build it and I helped take it away.

What advice would you give to someone who wanted to do your job? You need to be strong, really strong. You have to be OK with height. It usually takes about a year to get used to it. You can't work and hold on with one hand all the time. Many guys try it once, then back off and say, "This is not for me."

VOCABULARY
Phrasal verbs

> ⚠ **1** There are many examples of phrasal verbs in the reading texts on pages 54–55.
> I **came across** an ad …
> It's exciting to **end up** in different cities …
> Find more examples.
>
> **2** Some phrasal verbs are literal and some are idiomatic.
> Literal: She **looked out** the window at the sunset.
> Idiomatic: **Look out**! That dog's going to bite!
>
> ▶▶ **Grammar Reference 7.4 p. 146**

looking forward to
GONE OUT
get out of
back of
run out of
take off
END UP **look out!**
cut off
some up wit
came
get
across
put up with
looked out

1 In these pairs of sentences, one meaning of the phrasal verb is literal and the other is idiomatic. Say which is which.

1. a. The plane has just *taken off*. **idiomatic**
   b. Please *take off* your coat and sit down. **literal**
2. a. Oh, no! The lights have *gone out* again.
   b. If you *go out*, take an umbrella. It's going to rain.
3. a. (On the phone) Hello? Hello? I can't hear you. I think we've been *cut off*.
   b. She *cut off* a big piece of meat and gave it to the dog.
4. a. She *looked up* and smiled.
   b. I *looked up* the word in the dictionary.
5. a. Can you *pick up* my pen for me? It's under your chair.
   b. I *picked up* some Italian when I was working in Rome.

2 Replace the word in *italics* with the pronoun.
1. He turned on *the light*. **He turned it on.**
2. I came across *the ad*. **I came across it.**
3. She's taken off *her boots*.
4. He took up *golf* when he retired.
5. I get along well with *my parents*.
6. I'm looking for *my glasses*.
7. I looked up *the words* in my dictionary.
8. The waiter took away *the dirty plates*.

3 Complete each pair of sentences below with one of the phrasal verbs from the box.

> get along with   put up with   run out of
> looking forward to   come up with

1. How do you manage to _____ the noise from your neighbors?
   Some parents have to _____ bad behavior from their kids.
2. I'm broke. I have to _____ an idea for making money.
   We need to _____ a solution to this problem.
3. Has the photocopier _____ paper again?
   The children always _____ school as soon as the bell rings.
4. How well do you _____ your colleagues?
   I really don't _____ my teacher. She's too strict.
5. She's _____ going on vacation.
   We're _____ meeting you very much.

In which pairs of sentences above is the meaning different?

LISTENING AND SPEAKING
The busy life of a retired man

1 Work in groups and discuss the questions.

- Is anyone in your family retired? Who?
- What job did they do before retiring?
- How old were they when they retired? How long have they been retired?
- What do they do now?

2 **T 7.6** Look at the photograph of Lou Norris and his granddaughter, Patti. Lou used to be an engineer for Siemco Engineering in Indiana. Now he is retired. Listen to them talking.

Who do you think is happier, Lou or Patti? Why?

3 Underline the verbs. Then answer the questions.

1. How long *was he / has he been* retired?
2. How long *did he work / has he worked* for Siemco Engineering?
3. How long *was he married / has he been married*?
4. Who *did he go / has he gone* to Florida with?

4 Answer the questions.

1. Why does he like playing golf?
2. Which places has he visited since he retired? Where did he go last month?
3. Who are these people?
   - Bobby
   - Eric
   - Ted
   - Jessica
   - Marjorie
   - Miriam
4. What are the two sad events that Lou mentions?
5. What does Patti complain about?

What do you think?

- What is the usual retirement age for men and women in your country?
- What do you think is the best age to retire?
- When would you like to retire?
- What would you like to do when you retire?

EVERYDAY ENGLISH
Leaving a phone message

1 Complete the conversations with phrases from the box.

Let me give you my number	I'll call back later
I'm just returning his call	He's in a meeting
She's away from her desk	He's on another line

1. **A** Hello. May I speak to Arthur Lee, please?
   B I'm sorry. <u>He's in a meeting</u> right now. Can I take a message?
   A Yes. This is Pam Haddon. Mr. Lee called me earlier and left a message. _____ . Can you please tell him that I'm back in my office now?

2. **A** Hello. This is Ray Gervin. May I speak to Janet Wolf, please?
   B I'm sorry, Mr. Gervin. _____ at the moment. Would you like Ms. Wolf to call you when she gets back?
   A Yes. If you don't mind. _____ . It's 619-555-3153.

3. **A** Hello. May I speak to Douglas Ryan, please?
   B One moment, please. ... I'm sorry, but _____ . Do you want to hold?
   A No. That's OK. _____ .

2 **T 7.7** Listen and check. Practice the conversations with a partner.

8 Just imagine!

Conditionals · Time clauses · Base and strong adjectives · Making suggestions

TEST YOUR GRAMMAR

1 Match a line in **A** with a line in **B**.

If I had $5 million, I'd quit my job and travel around the world.

A	B
1. If I had $5 million,	I'll tell her the news.
2. If you're going to the post office,	I'd quit my job and travel around the world.
3. If I see Anna,	you have to work hard.
4. If you want to do well in life,	go to bed and rest.
5. If you don't feel well,	could you mail this letter for me?

2 What verb forms are used in the two parts of each sentence?

JIM GOES BACKPACKING
First conditional and time clauses

1 **T 8.1** Jim is going to backpack around Europe with his friend, Frank. Jim's mother is very worried. Listen and complete the conversation with the verbs from the box.

will you do   won't get   'll be (x2)   'll get
'll ask   won't do   get (x2)

Mom Oh, dear, I hope everything will be all right. You've never been out of the country before.

Jim Don't worry, Mom. I _'ll be_ OK. I can take care of myself. Anyway, I _____ with Frank. We _____ anything stupid.

Mom But what _____ if you run out of money?

Jim We _____ jobs, of course!

Mom Oh? What if you _____ lost?

Jim Mom! If we _____ lost, we _____ someone for directions, but we _____ lost because we know where we're going!

Mom Well, OK. ... But what if you ... ?

Practice the conversation in pairs.

2 Have more conversations between Jim and his mother.
What will you do if you ... ?

- get food poisoning
- lose your passport
- get sunburned
- get homesick
- get mugged
- don't like the food
- don't understand the language
- don't get along with Frank
- fall in love with some girl

> *What will you do if you get food poisoning?*

> *Don't worry, Mom. I'll ...*

3 **T 8.2** Listen to the next part of their conversation and put the verb into the correct tense.

Mom But how will we know if you're all right?

Jim When we ___get___ (get) to a city, I _____ (send) you an e-mail.

Mom But, Jim, it's such a long flight to Madrid!

Jim Look, as soon as we _____ (arrive) in Spain, I _____ (call) you.

Mom I _____ (be) worried until I _____ (hear) from you.

Jim I'll be OK. Really!

GRAMMAR SPOT

1 Which sentence expresses a future certainty, and which a future possibility?

   If we run out of money, we'll get jobs.
   When we get to a city, I'll send you an e-mail.

2 Underline the time expressions in the following sentences:

   When we get to a city, we'll send you an e-mail.
   As soon as we arrive, we'll call you.
   I'll be worried until I hear from you.

▶▶ **Grammar Reference 8.1 and 8.2 p. 147**

PRACTICE

The interview

1 Put *if*, *as soon as*, or *before* into each box. Put the verb into the correct tense.

Joe Bye, Honey! Good luck with the interview!

Sue Thanks. I'll need it. I hope the trains are running on time. ⬛ If ⬛ I ___'m___ (be) late for the interview, I _____ (be) furious with myself!

Joe Just stay calm! Call me when you can.

Sue I will. I _____ (call) you on my cell phone ⬛ _____ ⬛ I _____ (get) out of the interview.

Joe When _____ you _____ (know) ⬛ _____ ⬛ you have the job?

Sue They _____ (tell) me in the next few days. ⬛ _____ ⬛ they _____ (offer) me the job, I _____ (accept) it. You know that, don't you?

Joe Sure. But we'll worry about that later.

Sue OK. Are you going to work now?

Joe Well, I _____ (take) the kids to school ⬛ _____ ⬛ I _____ (go) to work.

Sue Don't forget to pick them up ⬛ _____ ⬛ you _____ (come) home.

Joe Don't worry, I won't forget. You'd better get going. ⬛ _____ ⬛ you _____ (not hurry), you _____ (miss) the train.

Sue OK. I _____ (see) you this evening. Bye!

T 8.3 Listen and check. Practice the conversation with a partner.

2 In pairs, ask and answer questions about the conversation with a partner.

• How/Sue/feel/if/late for the interview?

> *How will Sue feel if she's late for the interview?*

>> *She'll be furious with herself.*

• When/call/Joe?
• When/know/if/she has the job?
• What/she/do/if/they/offer her the job?
• What/Joe/do/before/go to work?
• When/pick up the kids?

WINNING THE LOTTERY
Second conditional

1 **T 8.4** Listen to five people saying what they would do if they won $5 million in the lottery. Who says what? Write a number, *1–5*.

2 Complete the sentences from the interviews.

1. I **'d give** a load of money to charity.
   I _____ my own island in the Caribbean.
2. I _____ it all on myself. Every last cent!
3. I _____ lots of land, so I _____ peace and quiet.
4. I _____ a space tourist and fly to Mars on the space shuttle.
5. I _____ my job and travel. But it _____ me.

Practice the sentences.

GRAMMAR SPOT

1 Look at the conditional sentences.

If **I have** time, **I'll do** some shopping.
If **I had** $5 million, **I'd buy** an island.

Which sentence expresses a possible situation? Which sentence expresses an unlikely situation, a dream?

2 We use the past tense and *would* to show unreality. The situation is contrary to facts.

If I had a lot of money, I'd travel around the world. (But I don't have a lot of money.)

▶▶ **Grammar Reference 8.3 and 8.4 p. 147**

PRACTICE

Group discussion

1 Work in groups to complete the questions. What would *you* do with $5 million? Ask and answer questions.

- What ... buy? **What would you buy?**
- How much ... give away? Who ... give it to?
- ... travel? Where ... to?
- What about your job? ... keep on working or ... quit your job?
- ... go on a spending spree, or ... invest the money?
- ... be happier than you are now?

Conversations with *will* and *would*

2 Look at the situations. Decide if they are possible or unlikely.

1. There's a good movie on TV tonight. **Possible**
2. You find a burglar in your home. **Unlikely**
3. You see a ghost.
4. Your friend isn't doing anything this weekend.
5. You are president of your country.
6. You don't have any homework tonight.
7. You can speak perfect English.

3 Ask and answer questions about what you will do or would do.

> *What will you do if there's a good movie on TV tonight?*

> *I'll watch it.*

> *What would you do if you found a burglar in your home?*

> *I'd call the police.*

Conditional forms

4 Match a line in **A** with a line in **B** and a sentence in **C**.

A	B	C
1. If Tony calls,	don't wait for me.	It would be really useful for work.
2. If you've finished your work,	I might take an evening class.	He can reach me there.
3. If I'm not back by 8 P.M.,	you have to have a visa.	Keep warm and drink plenty of fluids.
4. If you have the flu,	please let me know.	I'd love to show you around.
5. If you're ever in Vancouver,	tell him I'm at Alex's.	Just be back in 15 minutes.
6. If you go to Brazil,	you can take a break.	I'd love to learn more about photography.
7. I'd buy a computer	if I could afford it.	You can get one at the embassy.
8. If I had more time,	you should go to bed.	Go without me and I'll meet you at the party.

T 8.5 Listen and check. Practice the sentences.

5 Look at these three questions.
- What do you do if you can't get to sleep at night?
- What will you do if the weather's nice this weekend?
- What would you do if you found a wallet with a lot of money in it?

In groups, discuss how you would answer these questions.

READING AND SPEAKING
Who wants to be a millionaire?

1 **T 8.6** Listen to the song "Who Wants to Be a Millionaire?"
   - What don't the singers want to do?
   - What do the singers want to do?

   The tapescript is on page 129. Listen again and check.

2 Look at the chart below. Do you think these are good (✓) or
   bad (✗) suggestions for people who win a lot of money? Add
   your opinions to the chart.

If you win a lot of money, ...	Your opinion	The article's opinion
1. you should quit your job.	☐	☐
2. you should buy a new house.	☐	☐
3. you shouldn't tell anyone.	☐	☐
4. you should give money to everyone who asks for it.	☐	☐
5. you should go on a spending spree.	☐	☐
6. you should give away lots of it.	☐	☐

3 Read the article. What does it say about the six suggestions
   in Exercise 2? Put (✓) or (✗) in the chart.

4 These phrases have been taken out of the text. Where do
   they go?
   a. his unluckiest bet
   b. to move to a bigger house
   c. we feel at home
   d. among all the members of his family
   e. what the money would do to us
   f. as soon as possible
   g. most of their money will be spent
   h. nothing but misery

5 Answer the questions.
   1. According to the article, is it a good thing or a bad thing
      to win a lot of money?
   2. How does winning a large amount of money affect our
      work? Our home? Our friends? Our relatives?
   3. In what way is our life like a jigsaw? How does a windfall
      smash the jigsaw?
   4. How can money be wasted?
   5. What are the two bad luck stories?
   6. What made Jim Calhoun happy?
   7. How has Michael Kovaleski survived?

What do you think?

- How would you answer the questions in the last paragraph of
  the reading?
- What advice would you give to someone who has won a lot
  of money?

All over the world, lotteries create new millionaires every week. But what is it actually like to wake up one day with more money than you can imagine?

Nearly all of us have fantasized about winning the big
prize in a lottery. We dream about what we would do with
the money, but we rarely stop to think about
(1) _____e_____ !

For most of us, our way of life is closely linked to our
economic circumstances. The different parts of our lives fit
together like a jigsaw—work, home, friends, hobbies, and
sports make up our world. This is where we belong and
where (2) _____ . A sudden huge windfall would
dramatically change it all and smash the jigsaw.

For example, most people like the idea of not having
to work, but winners have found that without work there
no purpose to their day and no reason to get up in the
morning. It is tempting (3) _____ in a wealthy
neighborhood, but in so doing, you leave old friends and
routines behind.

Winners are usually advised not to publicize their
address and phone number, but charity requests and
begging letters still arrive. If they are not careful,
(4) _____ on lawyers' fees to protect them from
demanding relatives, guards to protect their homes and
swimming pools, and psychiatrists to protect their sanity!

Winners who lost it all

There are many stories about people who couldn't
learn how to be rich. In 1999 **Abby Wilson** from Lake City
Minnesota, won $14 million on Powerball, and it brought
her (5) _____ . She immediately went on a
spending spree that lasted for four years and five
marriages. She is now broke and alone. "I'm a miserable

Who wants to be a millionaire? We do.

person," she says. "Winning that money was the most awful thing that happened to me."

Then there is the story of **William Church,** 37, a cafeteria cook from Boston. He won the Massachusetts lottery, but it turned out to be (6) _____ . Three weeks after winning, he dropped dead of a heart attack, brought on by ceaseless hounding from the press, the public, and relatives, after his $3.6 million win was made public.

Winners who survived

For some people, the easiest thing is to get rid of the money (7) _____ . **Jim Calhoun,** a seaman from Canada, won $2 million, and blew the money in 77 days. He withdrew thousands of dollars a day from the bank and handed it to former shipmates and strangers in the street. On one occasion, he handed out $150,000 to homeless people in a Toronto park. Later he said he had no regrets about his wasted fortune.

Michael Kovaleski was the biggest lottery winner at the time when he won $40 million in the Illinois lottery. It has taken him years to get used to the changes in his life. "I couldn't have done it without my family," he says. "There were so many lies about me in the press. They said I had dumped my girlfriend, bought an island in the Caribbean, and become a drug addict. All wrong." His fortune has been divided (8) _____ .

A final thought

When you next buy a lottery ticket, just stop for a minute and ask yourself why you're doing it. Do you actually *want* to win? Or are you doing it for the excitement of *thinking about* winning?

Language work

The words in **A** are from the text. Match them with their definitions in **B**.

A	B
1. begging	dreamed
2. linked	took out
3. fantasized	connected
4. smash	an unexpected sum of money you receive
5. tempting	break violently
6. withdrew	attractive, inviting
7. broke	asking for something very strongly
8. windfall	having no money

VOCABULARY AND SPEAKING
Base adjectives and strong adjectives

1 Some adjectives have the idea of *very*. Look at these examples from the article on page 62.

a huge windfall   = a very big windfall
a miserable person = a very unhappy person

2 Put a base adjective from the box next to a strong adjective below.

good   bad   frightened   dirty   funny   tasty   hungry
tired   pretty/attractive   happy   surprised   angry

Base adjective	Strong adjective
good	great, wonderful, fantastic, superb
_____	exhausted
_____	delicious
_____	filthy
_____	terrified
_____	starving
_____	horrible, awful, terrible, disgusting
_____	thrilled, delighted
_____	astonished, amazed
_____	hilarious
_____	beautiful, gorgeous
_____	furious

> ❗ 1 We can make adjectives more extreme with adverbs such as *very* and *absolutely*.
>
> Their house is **very** big.
> Their backyard is **absolutely** enormous.
>
> 2 We can use *very* only with base adjectives.
> very tired   NOT ~~very exhausted~~
>
> 3 We can use *absolutely* only with strong adjectives.
> absolutely wonderful   NOT ~~absolutely good~~
>
> 4 We can use *really* with both base and strong adjectives.
> really tired   really exhausted

3 **T 8.7** Listen to the conversations and write down the adjectives and adverbs you hear. What do they refer to?

1.   *good, absolutely superb*   *movie*
2. _____   _____
3. _____   _____
4. _____   _____
5. _____   _____
6. _____   _____

LISTENING
Charity appeals

1 Work with a partner. Look at the list of charities and charitable causes below. Pick three of the charities and discuss why you think people should donate to them. Compare your answers with other pairs.

- a charity that helps elderly people with food and housing
- a hospice for people who are dying of an incurable disease
- an organization that provides emergency supplies and medicine for disaster victims
- a charity that helps homeless people
- cancer research
- a charity that helps people with AIDS
- animal shelters

2 **T 8.8** Listen to information about three charities and complete the chart.

- Who or what does the charity try to help?
- How does the charity help?

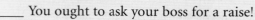

Save the Children®

	Who or what the charity tries to help	How the charity helps
1		
2		
3		

What do you think?

Imagine that you have $10,000 that you want to give to charity. Who would you give the money to? How would you divide it?

Think about what you would do, and then discuss your ideas with a partner.

If I had $10,000 to give away, I'd give it to three charities ...

WRITING: Words that join ideas
▶▶ Go to page 117

EVERYDAY ENGLISH
Making suggestions

1 Maria is bored and Paul is broke. Look at the suggestions made by their friends. Are they talking to Maria or Paul? Write **M** or **P**.

I'm bored!

I'm broke!

_M_ Let's go shopping!

____ If I were you, I'd get a better job.

____ Why don't you ask your parents?

____ You ought to ask your boss for a raise!

____ Why don't we go for a walk?

____ I don't think you should spend so much.

____ How about watching TV?

____ You'd better get a loan from the bank.

Which suggestions include the speaker?

2 **T 8.9** Listen to Maria and Paul and their friends. How can we make suggestions in English?

3 Listen again and read the tapescript on page 130. Notice how we accept and reject suggestions.

Work in pairs. Practice the conversations. Take turns covering the page.

Role play

4 Work in pairs. Make conversations for the situations, using different ways of making suggestions.

- You have a terrible cold.

A My head is killing me! And my nose is running!
B I think you should go to bed with a hot drink.
A That's a good idea. I'll go right now.
B How about a hot lemon drink? I'll make it for you.
A Oh, that would be great!

- You both have the evening free, and there's nothing good on TV.
- Your best friend is having a birthday party next week. You don't know what to give your friend as a gift.
- Your neighbor leaves his dog home alone every night while he's at work. The dog barks all the time when there's nobody home, and the noise is keeping you awake.
- Your apartment is a mess, the carpets and drapes are ragged, and the furniture is ancient. Suddenly, you inherit some money!
- You've been invited to a "potluck dinner" at an American friend's home. Each guest brings a dish of food to contribute, and you are supposed to bring a main dish.

9 Relationships

Modal verbs 2 — probability · Character adjectives · *So do I! Neither do I!*

TEST YOUR GRAMMAR

1 Read each pair of sentences. If the sentence is a fact, put (✓). If the sentence is only a possibility, put (?).

1. ☑ I'm in love!
   ⁇ I must be in love!
2. ☐ She could be taking a shower.
   ☐ She's taking a shower.
3. ☐ That isn't your bag.
   ☐ That can't be your bag.
4. ☐ You must have met my brother.
   ☐ You've met my brother.
5. ☐ They haven't met the president.
   ☐ They can't have met the president.
6. ☐ Shakespeare might have lived there.
   ☐ Shakespeare lived there.

Shakespeare might have lived there.

FOR SALE

2 Which sentences talk about the present? Which talk about the past?

I NEED HELP!
must be, could be, might be, can't be

1 Do you ever read advice columns in magazines or newspapers? What kind of problems do people often write about?

2 Lucy and Pam have problems. They wrote about them to "Debbie's Problem Page" in *Metro Magazine*. Read Debbie's advice.

Debbie's Problem Page

Lucy's problem:

"I think about him night and day!"

Debbie replies:

Hi Lucy,

Everyone has daydreams and there's nothing wrong with that. It's only a problem when you forget where dreams end and the real world begins. Don't write to him anymore. You know in reality that a relationship with him is impossible, and that running away to Hollywood is a crazy idea. You need to find other interests and friends your own age to talk to. Sitting at home watching him on TV won't help you. Your parents are clearly too busy to notice or listen. Your future is in your hands, so get a life, study hard, and good luck!

Yours,

Debbie

3 Look at Debbie's replies. Say who *he*, *she*, or *they* refer to in these sentences.

1. She must be exhausted. **Pam**
2. She must be in love with a movie star.
3. She could be a doctor or a nurse.
4. She can't be very old.
5. He must be unemployed.
6. She can't have many friends.
7. He might be a problem gambler.
8. They can't have much money.

4 Give reasons for each statement. Discuss with the class.
Pam must be exhausted because she works hard and she does all the housework.

5 Read Lucy and Pam's letters to Debbie on page 104 to find out if your ideas are correct.

GRAMMAR SPOT

1 The following sentences all express *It's possible that she's in love*. Which sentence is the most sure? Which sentences are less sure?

She **must be** in love.
She **might be** in love.
She **could be** in love.

2 How do we express *I **don't** think it's possible that she's in love*?

▶▶ **Grammar Reference 9.1 p. 148**

Pam's problem:

"We don't communicate anymore!"
Debbie replies:

Hi Pam,

You're not helping your marriage by saying nothing to him. He doesn't seem to notice how you feel. I know he's worried about his mother, but it's unfair that he's always at her house and leaves you to do all the housework. You have a tiring and stressful job, caring for sick people all day. You must make him understand this and ask him about the hundreds of lottery tickets you found. Encourage him to look for work—he'd feel better about himself if he had a job. In the meantime, don't hide your feelings; otherwise your anger and resentment will grow.

Yours,

Debbie

PRACTICE

Grammar and speaking

1 Respond to the statements or questions using the words in parentheses.

1. I haven't eaten anything since breakfast. (must, hungry)
   You must be hungry.
2. Bob works three jobs. (can't, much free time)
3. The phone's ringing. (might, Jane)
4. Paula's umbrella is soaking wet! (must, raining)
5. Listen to all those fire engines! (must, somewhere)
6. I don't know where Sam is. (could, his bedroom)
7. Marta isn't in the kitchen. (can't, cooking dinner)
8. Whose coat is this? (might, John's)

T 9.1 Listen and check. Practice the sentences with a partner.

What are they talking about?

2 **T 9.2** Listen to five short conversations and guess the answers to the questions below. Work with a partner.

> *It's Father's Day next Sunday.*

> *I know. Should we buy Dad a present or just send him a card?*

Conversation 1:
Who do you think they are? Friends? Brother and sister? Husband and wife?

They can't be just friends. They could be brother and sister. They might be husband and wife.

Conversation 2:
Where do you think the people are? At home? In a hotel? In a restaurant?

Conversation 3:
What do you think his job is? A truck driver? A taxi driver? An actor?

Conversation 4:
What do you think she's talking about? Taking a test? Adopting a baby? A job interview?

Conversation 5:
Who or what do you think they are talking about? A cat? A dog? A baby?

Who's who in the family?

Work in small groups. Go to page 105.

A VACATION WITH FRIENDS
must have been / can't have been

1 **T 9.3** Andy is calling Carl. In pairs, read and listen to Andy's side of the conversation. What do you think they are talking about?

- Hi! Carl? It's Andy. How are you? Doing better?

- Really? Still on crutches, eh? So you're not back at work yet?

- Another week! Is that when the cast comes off?

- I'm fine. We're both fine. Julie sends her love, by the way.

- Yes, yes, we have. Julie picked them up today. They're good. I didn't realize we'd taken so many of us all.

- Yes, the sunset? It's beautiful. All of us together on Bob and Marcia's balcony, with the mountains and the snow in the background. It brings back memories.

- Yes, I know. I'm sorry. But at least it happened at the end; it could have been the first day. You only missed the last two days.

- Yeah, and it was noisy too! We didn't have any views of the mountains from our room. Yeah, we've written. We e-mailed the manager yesterday, but I don't know if we'll get any money back.

- Yeah. The airline found it and put it on the next flight. Marcia was very relieved.

- Absolutely. It was a *great* vacation. Some ups and downs, but we all had fun. Should we go again next year?

- Great! It's a date. Next time go around the trees! I'll call you again soon, Carl. Take care!

- Bye.

2 Read the questions. Put (✓) next to the sentence you think is possible. Put (✗) next to the one you think is not possible.

1. What is the relationship between Andy and Carl?
   - ✓ They must be friends.
   - ✗ They could be business colleagues.

2. Where have they been?
   - ☐ They could have been on a skiing vacation.
   - ☐ They can't have been on a skiing vacation.

3. What happened to Carl?
   - ☐ He must have broken his leg.
   - ☐ He might have broken his arm.

4. How many people went on vacation?
   - ☐ There must have been four.
   - ☐ There might have been five or more.

5. Where did they stay?
   - ☐ They could have stayed with friends.
   - ☐ They must have stayed at a hotel.

6. What did they do on vacation?
   - ☐ They must have taken a lot of photos.
   - ☐ They can't have taken any photos.

7. Why did Andy and Julie send an e-mail to the manager?
   - ☐ They could have written to thank him.
   - ☐ They might have written to complain about their room.

8. What did Marcia lose?
   - ☐ It might have been her skis.
   - ☐ It could have been her suitcase.

3 Use some of the ideas in sentences 1–8 to say what you think happened to Andy and Carl.

Andy and Carl must be friends and they could have been on ...

4 **T 9.4** Listen to the full conversation between Andy and Carl. Which of your ideas were correct?

GRAMMAR SPOT

1 What is the past tense of these sentences?

| She | must can't could might | be on vacation. |

2 What is the past tense of these sentences?
- I must buy some sunglasses.
- I have to go home early.
- I can see the mountains from my room.

▶▶ **Grammar Reference 9.2 p. 148**

PRACTICE

Grammar and speaking

1 Respond to the statements or questions using the words in parentheses.

1. I can't find my ticket. (must, drop)
   You must have dropped it.
2. Mark didn't come to school last week. (must, sick)
3. Why is Isabel late for class? (might, oversleep)
4. I can't find my homework. (must, forget)
5. The teacher's checking Maria's work. (can't, finish already)
6. How did Bob get such a good grade on that test? (must, cheat)

T 9.5 Listen and check. Practice the sentences with a partner.

Discussing grammar

2 Here is a list of modal auxiliary verbs. How many can you fit naturally into each blank? Discuss as a class the differences in meaning.

| can | can't | could | must | might | should |

1. He _____ have been born during World War II.
2. _____ you help me with the dishes, please?
3. You _____ see the doctor immediately.
4. It _____ be raining.
5. _____ we go out for dinner tonight?
6. I _____ stop smoking.
7. It _____ have been Bill that you met at the party.
8. I _____ learn to speak English.

READING AND SPEAKING
A father and daughter

1 Talk about these questions with a partner and then with the class.
   - Who do you look more like, your mother or your father?
   - Who are you more like in character, your mother or your father?
   - Do you want to raise your children in the same way you were raised?

2 In the magazine article on the right, two different members of the same family describe their relationship with each other.

   Divide into two groups.

   Group A Read what Oliver Darrow says about his daughter, Carmen.

   Group B Read what Carmen Darrow says about her father, Oliver.

3 Discuss in your groups the answers to the questions about your person.
   1. Which two sentences best describe their relationship?
      a. It was closer when Carmen was a child.
      b. They get along well and have similar interests.
      c. They don't have much in common.
   2. Which two sentences best describe Oliver?
      a. He's done a lot for his daughter.
      b. He isn't very sensitive to how she feels.
      c. He's more interested in himself than his family.
   3. Which two sentences best describe Carmen?
      a. She is selfish and spoiled.
      b. She tried to please her father.
      c. She was never really happy until she married George.
   4. How did Oliver behave in front of Carmen's friends?
   5. Why did she leave school?
   6. Is she happily married? How do you know?
   7. What does Carmen think of her father's career?
   8. Why don't they see each other very much?

FAMILY MATTERS

Two points of view on a family relationship

OLIVER DARROW, actor, talks about his daughter, Carmen.

"My first wife and I only had one child. It might have been nice to have more. I would have liked a son, but we just had Carmen.

I see her as my best friend. I think she always comes to me first if she has a problem. We have the same sense of humor and share many interests, except that she's crazy about animals, obsessed with them—she has always had dogs, cats, and horses in her life.

We were closest when she was about four, which I think is a wonderful age for a child. That's when they need their parents most. But as soon as Carmen went to school, she seemed to grow up and grow apart from her family, and any father finds it difficult with a teenage daughter. She was very moody and had an odd group of friends. There was an endless stream of strange young men coming to our house. I remember I once got annoyed with her in front of her friends and she didn't talk to me for days.

"I see her as my best friend."

I've always wanted the best for her. We sent her to a good school, but she wasn't happy there. She left because she wanted to become an actress, so with my connections I got her into drama school, but she didn't like that either. She worked for a while doing small roles in movies, but she must have found it boring because she gave it up, though she never really said why. She got married a few years ago; her husband's a veterinarian. They must be happy because they work together, and she loves animals.

We have the same tastes in books and music. When she was younger, I used to take her to the opera—that's my passion—but she can't have liked it very much because she hasn't come with me for years. I don't think she goes to the movies or watches TV much. She might watch my movies, but I don't know. It's not the kind of thing she talks to me about.

I'm very pleased to have Carmen. She's a good daughter, but I don't think she likes my new wife very much because she doesn't visit very often. I'm looking forward to being a grandfather someday. I hope she'll have a son."

CARMEN DARROW, an assistant vet in Vermont, talks about her father, Oliver.

"I don't really know my father. He isn't easy to get along with. I've always found him difficult to talk to. He's kind of reserved, but he loves to be recognized and asked for his autograph. I think people see his movies and think he's very easygoing, but he really isn't. He's won some awards for his movies, and he's really proud of them. He used to show them to my friends when they came to the house and that really embarrassed me.

He can't have been home much when I was a small child because I don't remember much about him. He mostly stayed away from family life. His work always came first, and he was often away from home making movies. I wasn't surprised when he and my mother split up.

He must have wanted the best for me, but the best was always what *he* wanted. He chose my school and I hated it. I had no friends there, I was miserable and didn't do well, so I was asked to leave. He must have been very disappointed, but he said nothing to me. He wanted me to be an actor like him but I'm not at all like him. I tried it for a while, but I was miserable until I met my husband. He's a veterinarian and I'm his assistant. I'm now doing what I always wanted to do, work with animals.

My father and I have always been so different. I love animals and he loves books and music, and above all opera, which I hate. If he

> ## "He's like a stranger."

comes to see us (we live on a farm), he always wears the totally wrong clothes, but we don't see much of each other these days. It's because he really didn't want me to marry George. He wanted me to marry a famous movie star or something, but of course I didn't. George and I don't want children, we have our animals, but my father would love to have a grandson. Maybe his new wife will give him the son he wants, but probably not. She cares too much about being slim and beautiful.

I occasionally see one of his movies on TV. I find it hard to believe he's my father. He's like a stranger."

4 Find a partner from the other group and compare your answers. Then read the other text.

What do you think?

Who has the more realistic view of the relationship? Oliver or Carmen? Why?

Language work

Rewrite these sentences about Oliver and Carmen. Use the modal verb in parentheses in either the present or past and complete the sentence.

1. I'm sure Carmen likes animals a lot because … (must)
   She must like animals because she enjoys working with them.
2. I don't think Oliver is a very famous actor because … (can't)
3. I think maybe he has won an Academy Award® because … (might)
4. I'm sure she had a lot of friends when she was a teenager because … (must)
5. I don't think she worked hard in school because … (can't)

VOCABULARY AND SPEAKING
Character adjectives

1 Take the personality quiz to discover what type of person you are. Use a dictionary to check any new words. Write **Y** for *Yes*, **N** for *No*, and **S** for *Sometimes*.

What type of person are YOU?

1 Are you usually smiling and happy? ☐

2 Do you enjoy the company of other people? ☐

3 Do you find it difficult to meet new people? ☐

4 Do you have definite plans for your future career? ☐

5 Does your mood change often and suddenly for no reason? ☐

6 Do you notice other people's feelings? ☐

7 Do you think the future will be good? ☐

8 Can your friends depend on you? ☐

9 Is your room often a mess? ☐

10 Do you get annoyed if you have to wait for anyone or anything? ☐

11 Do you put off until tomorrow what you could do today? ☐

12 Do you work hard? ☐

13 Do you keep your feelings and ideas to yourself? ☐

14 Do you often give presents? ☐

15 Do you talk a lot? ☐

16 Are you usually calm and not worried by things? ☐

2 Work with a partner. Ask your partner to take the quiz about *you*. Compare your ideas and your partner's ideas about you. Are they the same or different?

3 Match these adjectives with the questions in the quiz.

a. reliable   _8_
b. optimistic ____
c. sociable   ____
d. talkative   ____
e. reserved   ____
f. shy   ____
g. impatient   ____
h. ambitious   ____
i. lazy   ____
j. generous   ____
k. moody   ____
l. hardworking ____
m. easygoing   ____
n. messy   ____
o. cheerful   ____
p. sensitive   ____

4 Which are positive qualities and which are negative? Which could be both?

Positive	Negative	Both
reliable		

5 What is the opposite of each of the 16 adjectives in Exercise 3? Remember that the prefixes *in-* and *un-* can sometimes be used to make negatives. Which of the adjectives in Exercise 3 can use these?

unreliable

6 Describe someone in the class to your partner, but don't say who it is. Can your partner guess who it is?

LISTENING AND SPEAKING
Brothers and sisters

1 Do a class survey.
1. Find out who has any brothers and/or sisters.
2. Who has the most? How many? Do they like having lots of brothers and sisters?
3. Does anyone have a twin brother or sister? Do they like being a twin?
4. Is anyone in the class an only child? Do they like being an only child?

2 **T 9.6** Listen to two people talking about their families. Complete the chart.

	Luisa	Rose
1. How many brothers and sisters does she have?		
2. Was she happy as a child? Why or why not?		
3. Is she happy now? Why or why not?		
4. What do you learn about other members of her family?		

What do you think?

Discuss these questions.
- How many children do you have? / would you like to have?
- What size is the perfect family?
- Would you like to have twins?

WRITING: Beginning and ending letters
▶▶ Go to page 118

EVERYDAY ENGLISH
So do I! Neither do I!

1 **T 9.7** Listen to Sue. She is at a party and her friends are talking about themselves. Put a ✓ if Sue agrees with them and an ✗ if she disagrees.

Sue's friends	Sue	Sue's words
1. I want to travel the world.	✓	*So do I.*
2. I don't want to have lots of children.		
3. I can speak four languages.		
4. I can't drive.		
5. I'm not going to get married until I'm 35.		
6. I went to London last year.		
7. I've never been to Australia.		
8. I don't like politicians.		
9. I'm bored with Hollywood actors.		
10. I love going to parties.		

2 **T 9.7** Listen again and write the exact words Sue uses. Choose from the lists below.

So am I.	Neither am I.	I am.	I'm not.
So do I.	Neither do I.	I do.	I don't.
So can I.	Neither can I.	I can.	I can't.
So did I.	Neither did I.	I did.	I didn't.
So have I.	Neither have I.	I have.	I haven't.

Listen again and check your answers.

What does Sue say when it is the same for her?

What does she say when it is different?

▶▶ **Grammar Reference 9.3 and 9.4 p. 148**

3 Work in pairs. Read aloud the statements in Exercise 1 to each other and give the true response for you.

4 Go around the class. Everyone must make a statement about themselves or give an opinion about something. The others in the class must respond.

I love chocolate!

So do I. / Me too.

I don't!

I didn't do my homework.

Neither did I. / Me neither.

I did!

Present Perfect Continuous · Time expressions · Compound nouns · Quantity

TEST YOUR GRAMMAR

1 For each pair, match a line in **A** with a line or picture in **B**.

A	B
1. What do you do What are you doing	these days? for a living?
2. He speaks He's speaking	three languages. to the teacher.
3. She has She's having	a baby next month. a sister and a brother.
4. What have you done What have you been doing	with my pen? I can't find it. since I last saw you?

5. Who drank my soda?

Who's been drinking
my soda?

6. I read that book. I was reading that book	It was really good. when you called.

2 Look at the second verbs in each pair of sentences. What do they have in common?

TRY, TRY AGAIN
Present Perfect Continuous

1 Read the newspaper article. Answer the questions.
1. Why is Father Dan celebrating?
2. How long has he been learning to drive?
3. Was it easy?
4. How many lessons has he had?

Finally He Passes!

PRIEST PASSES DRIVING TEST AFTER 632 LESSONS OVER 17 YEARS

Father Daniel Hernandez is celebrating. He has finally passed his driving test. He has been learning to drive for the past 17 years, and he has had a total of 632 driving lessons.

Father Dan, 34, has spent over $15,000 on driving lessons, he has had 8 different instructors, and he has crashed his car 5 times. Then last week he finally managed to pass.

Father Dan, a parish priest in San Antonio, Texas, began driving at the age of 17. "My instructors have been telling me for years that I would never pass, but I was determined to prove them wrong."

Father Dan's luck changed when he took his test for the 56th time. He said, "When I was told that I'd passed, I got down on my knees and thanked God."

So how has he been celebrating? "I've been visiting all my friends and relatives and people who live in the small towns around here. I haven't seen some of them for years, because I haven't been able to get to them. Now I can go everywhere!"

2 Here are the answers to some questions. Write the questions using *he*.

1. Seventeen years. *(How long ... ?)*
   How long has he been learning to drive?
2. Six hundred thirty-two.
   (How many ... ?)
3. Over $15,000. *(How much ... ?)*
4. Eight. *(How many ... ?)*
5. Five times. *(How many times ... ?)*
6. When he was 17. *(When ... ?)*
7. Fifty-six times. *(How many ... ?)*
8. By visiting all his friends and relatives.
   (How ... ?)

T 10.1 Listen and check.

GRAMMAR SPOT

1 Find examples of the Present Perfect
Simple and the Present Perfect
Continuous in the text.

2 Look at the questions below. Which one
asks about an activity? Which one asks
about a quantity?

   How long have you been learning
   English?
   How many teachers have you had?

▶▶ **Grammar Reference 10.1–10.2 p. 149**

PRACTICE

Conversations

1 Write a question with *How long ... ?* Use either the Present Perfect Simple or the Present Perfect Continuous. (If both are possible, use the Continuous.)

1. I live in the country.   How long <u>have you been living in the country</u> ?
2. I play tennis.   How long _____ ?
3. I know Jack well.   How long _____ ?
4. I work in Hong Kong.   How long _____ ?
5. I have a Japanese car.   How long _____ ?

2 Make sentences with the same verbs about yourself. In pairs, ask and answer questions with *How long ... ?*

3 For each of the sentences in Exercise 1, write another question in the Past Simple.

1. When ____<u>did you</u>____ move there?
2. How old _____ when _____ started _____ ?
3. Where _____ meet _____ ?
4. Why _____ decide _____ ?
5. How much _____ pay _____ ?

4 **T 10.2** Read and listen to the conversation.

   A You look tired. What have you been doing?
   B I'm exhausted! I've been getting ready to go on vacation.
   A Have you done everything?
   B Well, I've packed the suitcases, but I haven't been to the bank yet.

Work in pairs. Make similar conversations.

1. **A** covered in paint/what/doing?
   B redecorating the bathroom.
   A finished yet?
   B painted the door/haven't put up the wallpaper yet.
2. **A** hands dirty/what/doing?
   B filthy/working in the garden.
   A finished yet?
   B cut the grass/haven't watered the flowers yet.
3. **A** your eyes are red/what/doing?
   B exhausted/studying for my final exams.
   A finished yet?
   B finished my chemistry and history/haven't started English yet.

T 10.3 Listen and check. Practice the conversations again.

Discussing grammar

5 Why are these sentences strange? What would be better?

1. Ouch! I've been cutting my finger.
2. "Why is your hair wet?" "I've swum."
3. You've got tears in your eyes. Why have you cried?
4. I'm really sorry, but I've been crashing into the back of your car.
5. I've written my autobiography this afternoon.

A WRITER'S LIFE
Time expressions

1 Ellen McDonald is a writer. Look at the chart of events in her life. Answer the questions.

1. Ellen has had an interesting life so far. What are some of the things she has done?
2. How long has she been writing?
3. What kinds of things has she written?
4. How many novels has she written?
5. Has she won any prizes for her writing?
6. How long has she been married to Jack?
7. How many times has she been married?
8. How long has she been writing her autobiography?

AGE	LIFE EVENT
0	Born on April 10, 1960, in Boston
6	Wrote short stories about animals
8	Collection of poems published in April 1968; visit to Ireland
11	September 16, 1971, mother died; visit to France and Spain
18–22	Went to Columbia University and majored in English literature
19	Met her first husband
21	Got married in spring 1981
22	Graduated with honors in June 1982 First novel, *Chains*, published in fall 1982
23	Daughter born June 14, 1983
25	Novel *Strangers in the Night*, 1985, won the National Book Award for best fiction
29	Divorced; visit to Vietnam, China, Japan
31	Bought a house in Greenwich, Connecticut
33	Novel *The Cry at Dawn* published
35–37	Wrote scripts for a TV series; met Jack, a TV producer
38	Got married on August 3, 1998, to Jack; moved to her current address in southern California
40	Won the Library Association Award for literary merit
42	Began her autobiography in 2002
Now	Still writing her autobiography

2 Complete the sentences with words from the box.

while she was in college	at the age of six
since she married Jack	two years after she got married
after the publication	until she married Jack
while she was working	between 1978 and 1982

1. She wrote her first stories __at the age of six__ .
2. _____ of a collection of poems in 1968, she went to Ireland.
3. She was at Columbia University _____ .
4. She met her first husband _____ .
5. Her daughter was born _____ .
6. She met Jack _____ on a TV series.
7. She lived in Greenwich, Connecticut, _____ .
8. She has been living in southern California _____ .

▶▶ **Grammar Reference 10.3 p. 149**

WRITING: Sentence combination
▶▶ Go to page 119

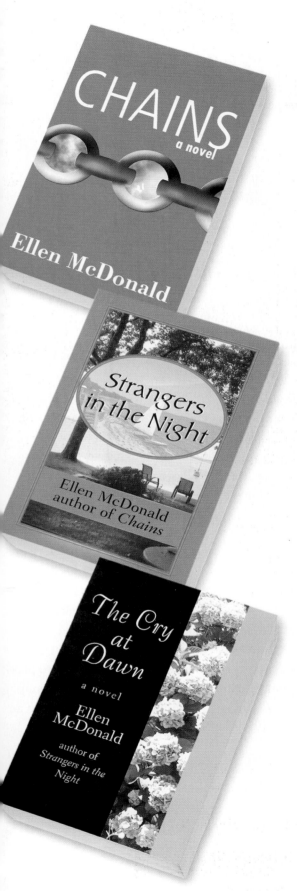

PRACTICE

Questions and answers

1 Ask and answer the questions about Ellen McDonald.

1. When ... born?

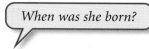

When was she born?

In 1960.

2. When ... collection of poems published?
3. When ... get married for the first time?
4. What ... major in at Columbia?
5. Which countries ... been to?
6. How long ... first marriage last?
7. When ... for the second time?
8. How long ... in southern California?

T 10.4 Listen and check.

2 Make a similar chart of the events of your life or the life of someone you know well. In pairs, ask and answer questions.

3 Ellen is on a two-week tour of England and Scotland. Look at her schedule.

	Week 1	Week 2
Sunday	London	Birmingham
Monday	London	Manchester
Tuesday	London	Manchester
Wednesday	London	Edinburgh
Thursday	Oxford	Edinburgh
Friday	Oxford	Edinburgh
Saturday	Birmingham	Fly home

4 It is Monday of the second week, and Ellen is at a press conference. How does she answer these questions?

1. How long are you here in Britain for? **Just two weeks.**
2. How long have you been in Britain? **Eight days.**
3. When do you go back to California?
4. Where were you the day before yesterday?
5. Where were you this time last week?
6. Where will you be the day after tomorrow?

T 10.5 Listen and check.

Discussing grammar

5 Correct the mistakes in the questions.

1. What time did you go to bed at last night?
2. What have you done last weekend?
3. What are you doing this night?
4. Are you going to study English the next month?
5. Have you been studying English since three years?
6. How long you live in this town?
7. When is your mother born?
8. How long have you been knowing your teacher?

6 Work with a partner. Ask and answer the questions in Exercise 5.

READING AND SPEAKING
A big name in Hollywood

1 Discuss the questions about your favorite movie actor or actress.

- What movies has he/she been in?
- What kind of movies does he/she act in? Action? Romance? Comedy?
- What is the best role he/she has ever played?
- What do you think he/she is like as a person? What does he/she look like?
- Where does he/she live?
- What do you know about his/her family?
- What is he/she most famous for? Looks? Acting ability? Behavior off-screen?

2 Match a line in **A** with a line in **B**.

A	B
1. She won	as the bad guy.
2. I was once	She has real talent.
3. In movies he is always cast	the big time.
4. She auditioned	a fake painting.
5. He's going to make	an award.
6. She was turned down	for the part of Mary. (x2)
7. Give her a break!	an extra in a movie.
8. I was sold	

3 Read the magazine article about Dennis Woodruff. Then answer the questions in Exercise 1 about Dennis.

4 Answer the questions.
1. Who will you probably not see if you go to Hollywood?
2. How does Dennis try to sell himself?
3. Is he famous?
4. Will he make the big time?
5. Where does he audition? How do people react?
6. Why is he tired?
7. How did he get the idea of promoting himself?
8. Is Dennis optimistic?

Famous for

I F YOU GO to Hollywood and look around the trendy coffee shops and restaurants, it is unlikely that you will meet your favorite movie star. However, it is almost certain that you will meet Dennis Woodruff.

Dennis is a movie star—well, sort of. You learn this quickly because he tells everyone he meets. He wears a T-shirt that says "Dennis Woodruff, world-famous actor." On his modified Chevrolet convertible he has five Oscars® (fake, unfortunately) and other awards that he has won. He also hands out videotapes of his movies in exchange for a modest $10.

If fame is a matter of being known by influential people, then Dennis Woodruff is certainly famous. He describes himself as Hollywood's best known out-of-work actor. He has been looking for work for 25 years. It is true that he has been on television over 300 times and done work in about 45 motion pictures, but invariably as an extra.

But mostly he is known as the hippie guy with the long blond ponytail, who is trapped in the only role he has been able to play with any success—playing Dennis. Everything about Dennis has to do with selling himself. He talks

not being famous

Dennis Woodruff, Hollywood movie star—sort of

constantly about his life, his talent, his artistic abilities, his ambitions. His never-ending search for work in the movie industry no longer has any realistic chance of success, so now he acts out the role of an actor looking for work. "Cast me!" shouts the writing on his car. "Buy my movie!"

"Actually," says Dennis, "I am a movie star. It's just that no one has realized it yet." His movies, titled *Dennis Woodruff the Movie, Parts I and II* and *Double Feature, starring Dennis Woodruff* are heavily autobiographical— more documentaries of his life than anything else. You can watch him auditioning for parts in front of the security cameras at local restaurants. People recognize him and then, sadly, ignore him.

He has rugged, unconventional good looks, though he seems tired. "I've been making another movie about me. It's called *Life Is Art*. I want to show everyone how my life is like a work of art."

One of the most miserable tales he tells is about how he nearly made the big time. The famous actor John Wayne was going to give him a break, but unfortunately he died. Legendary producer Otto Preminger wanted to make him a star. He also died.

Now nearly 50, Dennis first had the idea of promoting himself over 20 years ago when he asked a casting director why he had been turned down for a part. "Because you're not a big name in Hollywood," came the answer. Dennis immediately wrote his name in huge letters on the top of his car. It didn't get him any work, but it did get him noticed.

He's been living in a mobile home in East Hollywood for 30 years, and to his credit, he manages to earn a living. He has set up a production company with his brother, and he has sold 15,000 copies of his video. True success, he feels, is just around the corner. Now there's optimism for you.

Language work

5 Here are the answers to some questions. Write the questions.

1. **A** <u>How many fake Oscars®</u>
   <u>does he have?</u>
   B Five.
2. **A** _____ ?
   B For 25 years.
3. **A** _____ ?
   B Over 300 times.
4. **A** _____ ?
   B For 30 years.
5. **A** _____ ?
   B 15,000.

6 The words in **A** are in the text. Match them with similar meanings in **B**.

A	B
1. trendy	improbable
2. unlikely	not real
3. fake	caught so you can't move
4. trapped	pay no attention
5. ignore	different from what is considered usual
6. unconventional	stories
7. tales	enormous
8. huge	fashionable

VOCABULARY
Compound nouns

1 Nouns can be combined to make a new word or phrase. These are called compound nouns. They are written in different ways. Look at these words from the article about Dennis Woodruff.

One word	Two words
ponytail	coffee shop
videotape	movie star

2 Put one word in each box to form three compound nouns.

1
dining
bath   **room**
waiting

7
_____ brush
_____ stylist
_____ cut

2
_____ ache
_____ brush
_____ paste

8
_____ mail
_____ conditioning
_____ port

3
phone
fax _____
credit card

9
_____ cup
_____ shop
_____ pot

4
_____ director
_____ theater
_____ review

10
_____ set
_____ glasses
_____ tan

5
_____ place
_____ engine
_____ works

11
wrapping
writing _____
toilet

6
credit
birthday _____
business

12
_____ mall
_____ cart
_____ list

3 Here are definitions of some compound words from Exercise 2. What are the words?
1. A pain in your tooth or teeth
   toothache
2. A place where airplanes take off and land
3. A newspaper article that gives an opinion about a new movie
4. A person whose job is to cut and style people's hair
5. The time when the sun goes down and night begins
6. A large building or buildings with many stores, restaurants, etc.

4 Write similar definitions of other words from Exercise 2 and test your classmates.

LISTENING AND SPEAKING
Collectors

1 Discuss these questions as a class.
- What kinds of things do people often collect?
- Do you collect anything? Did you used to collect things when you were younger?
- Why do people collect things?

2 You are going to listen to two people who are both passionate collectors. Divide into two groups.

Group A `T 10.6` Listen to Andrea Levitt who collects dolls.

Group B `T 10.7` Listen to Jeff Parker who collects *Star Wars* memorabilia.

Look at the pictures of your person. What can you see? What does he/she collect? What questions would you like to ask him/her?

3 Answer the questions.
1. Where does he/she live? Who with?
2. What does he/she do for a living?
3. How long has he/she been collecting?
4. How many items has he/she collected?
5. How many rooms of the house are taken up with the collection?
6. What's his/her favorite item?
7. Where do the items come from?
8. Is he/she in touch with other people who share the same hobby?

4 Find a partner from the other group. Compare and exchange information.

Andrea Levitt and her doll collection

Jeff Parker and his *Star Wars* collection

EVERYDAY ENGLISH
Expressing quantity

1 Choose a word or words from the box to complete the sentences. Some are used more than once.

too much	a few	any	How many
as much as	some	How much	too many
	as many as	enough	a little

1. **A** _____ coffee do you drink?
   B At least six cups a day.
   A That's _____ . You shouldn't drink _____ that.

2. **A** Do we have _____ sugar?
   B Yes, but not _____ . We need _____ more.

3. **A** _____ do you earn?
   B Not _____ to pay all my bills!

4. **A** _____ people are there in your class?
   B Forty.
   A I think that's _____ .

5. **A** _____ aspirins do you usually take when you have a headache?
   B About four or five.
   A That's _____ . You shouldn't take _____ that!

6. **A** How old are you?
   B Seventeen. I'm old _____ to get married, but not old _____ to vote!

7. **A** When did you last go to the movies?
   B Pretty recently. Just _____ days ago.

8. **A** Do you take milk in your coffee?
   B Just _____ .

T 10.8 Listen and check. Practice the conversations with a partner.

2 In pairs, ask and answer the questions in Exercise 1.

11 Tell me about it!

Indirect questions · Question tags · The body · Informal language

TEST YOUR GRAMMAR

1 All of these sentences are correct. Why is there no *does* in sentences 2 and 3?

1. Where does she live?
2. I know where she lives.
3. Can you tell me where she lives?

2 Choose the correct question tag.

It's a beautiful day, isn't it?

1. It's a beautiful day,	did he?
2. You like learning English,	isn't it?
3. You've been to Australia,	don't you?
4. Henry didn't say that,	haven't you?

THE FIRST DAY OF VACATION
Indirect questions

1 **T 11.1** Flavia has just checked into her hotel in Toronto. Look at the information she wants, then listen to the conversation. Complete her sentences.

What Flavia wants to know	What Flavia says
1. Could you help me?	I wonder if _____ help me.
2. Are we near the CN Tower?	I'm not sure _____ near the CN Tower.
3. Are there any good restaurants nearby?	Can you tell me if _____ ?
4. When do the banks open?	I don't know when _____ .
5. Which restaurant did you suggest?	I'm sorry, but I can't remember which restaurant _____ .

2 Read the tapescript on page 133 and practice the conversation. Then close your books and do it again.

3 Here is some more information that Flavia wants to know. Use the prompts to ask indirect questions.

1. When was Toronto founded?
   (I wonder when …)
   I wonder when Toronto was founded.
2. What's the population of the city?
   (Do you know … ?)
3. Where can I exchange some money?
   (I'd like to know …)
4. What's the exchange rate today?
   (Do you happen to know … ?)
5. Is there a post office near here?
   (Could you tell me … ?)
6. Where is there a good place to buy souvenirs?
   (Do you have any idea … ?)

4 In pairs, ask and answer similar indirect questions about the city or town where you are now.

PRACTICE

Asking polite questions

1 Match a word in **A** with a line in **B** and a line in **C**.

A	B	C
What	newspaper	times have you been on a plane?
How	sports	do you follow?
Which	long	music do you like?
	far	do you read?
	kind of	is it to the station from here?
	many	time do you spend watching TV?
	much	does it take you to get ready in the morning?

2 In pairs, ask and answer indirect questions using the ideas in Exercise 1.

Could you tell me which sports you follow?

Would you mind telling me which newspaper you read?

Who was Walt Disney?

3 What do you know about Walt Disney?

He made cartoons and animated movies.

He built Disneyland.

4 Make sentences about Walt Disney using these beginnings and the prompts in 1–8 below.

I wonder …	I have no idea …
I'd like to know …	Does anybody know …

1. when … born

I wonder when he was born.

2. where … live as a child
3. how old … when … start … draw
4. if … any children
5. when the first Mickey Mouse movie … come out
6. if … won any Oscars®
7. when … the first Disneyland park … open
8. if … still alive

5 Work with a partner. You each have different information about Walt Disney. Ask and answer questions to complete the information.

Student A Go to page 106.
Student B Go to page 108.

WE LIKE ANIMALS, DON'T WE?

Question tags

1 **T 11.2** Listen to Gabriella, age 4, talking to her mother, Karen.

G Mommy?
K Yes, Gabby?
G I have ten fingers, don't I?
K Yes, that's right, Sweetie. Ten pretty little fingers.
G And Daddy didn't go to work this morning, did he?
K No, it's Saturday. He's working in the yard today.
G And we like animals, don't we, Mommy?
K Yes, we do. Especially our cats, Sammy and Teddy.
G Can I have a cookie now, Mommy?

2 **T 11.2** Listen again. Does Gabriella's intonation go up or down at the end of the sentences?

> ### GRAMMAR SPOT
>
> **1** Gabriella knows that she has ten fingers, and she knows that her father didn't go to work. Is Gabriella asking for information or just making conversation?
>
> **2** How do we form question tags?
>
> ▶▶ **Grammar Reference 11.2 p. 150**

3 Look at the conversation between Karen and her assistant. Fill in the blanks with a question tag from the box.

> didn't I?   isn't it?   am I?   don't I?

K Now, what's happening today? I have a meeting this afternoon, _____ ?
A Yes, that's right. With Henry and Tom.
K And the meeting's here, _____ ?
A No, it isn't. It's in Tom's office at 3 P.M.
K Oh! I'm not having lunch with anyone, _____ ?
A No, you're free for lunch.
K Phew! And I signed all my letters, _____ ?
A No, you didn't, actually. They're on your desk, waiting for you.
K OK. I'll do them now. Thanks a lot.

T 11.3 Listen and check. Practice the conversation with a partner.

> ### GRAMMAR SPOT
>
> **1** Did the intonation of Karen's question tags go up or down?
>
> **2** Which speaker, Karen or Gabriella, uses question tags to mean "I'm not sure, so I'm checking"?
>
> Which speaker, Karen or Gabriella, uses question tags to mean "Talk to me"?
>
> ▶▶ **Grammar Reference 11.2 p. 150**

PRACTICE

Question tags and intonation

1 Look at the sentences in the box and complete the question tags.

a.	It isn't very warm today, ___*is it?*___	↗
b.	You can cook, _____	
c.	You have a CD player, _____	
d.	Mary's very smart, _____	
e.	There are a lot of people here, _____	
f.	The movie wasn't very good, _____	
g.	I'm next in line, _____	
h.	You aren't going out dressed like that, _____	

2 **T 11.4** Listen and check. Write ↗ if the questions tag rises and ↘ if it falls.

3 Match a response with a sentence in Exercise 1.

- _d_ 1. Yes. She's extremely bright.
- ____ 2. Believe it or not, I don't. I have a cassette player, though.
- ____ 3. Why? What's wrong with my clothes? I thought I looked really cool.
- ____ 4. No, it's freezing.
- ____ 5. Yes, you are. You'll be called next.
- ____ 6. Me? No! I can't even boil an egg.
- ____ 7. I know! It's absolutely packed! I can't move!
- ____ 8. It was terrible! The worst I've seen in ages.

T 11.5 Listen and check. Practice the conversations with a partner.

Conversations

3 Add three question tags to the conversation below. Do they rise or fall?

A It's so romantic.
B What is?
A Well, they're really in love.
B Who?
A Paul and Mary.
B Paul and Mary aren't in love.
A Oh, yes, they are. They're crazy about each other.

T 11.6 Listen and compare your answers.

4 Choose one of the conversations on page 107 and add question tags. Learn it by heart, and act it out for the rest of the class.

5 **T 11.7** Listen and check. Are your ideas the same?

READING AND SPEAKING
How well do you know your world?

1 Do you know the answers to these questions?

- ○ Do animals have feelings?
- ● What are the Earth's oldest living things?
- ○ What is the most terrible natural disaster to have hit the Earth?
- ● Why isn't there a row 13 on airplanes?
- ○ Why do women live longer than men?
- ● What man-made things can be seen from space?
- ○ Was Uncle Sam a real person?

2 Put one of these lines before each question in Exercise 1. What is true for you?

> I think ...   I think I know ...   I'm not sure ...
> I don't know ...   I have no idea ...   I wonder ...

I think animals have feelings.

I have no idea what the Earth's oldest living things are.

Discuss your ideas as a class. Which question interests you the most?

3 Read the questions and answers from a science magazine. Here are the last lines of the seven texts. Which text do they go with?

a. The country with the highest life expectancy is Japan—84 years for women and 77 for men.

b. Less than 24 hours after the meal, Christ was crucified.

c. It is very likely that this explosion wiped out all the dinosaurs.

d. Fear is instinctive and requires no conscious thought.

e. You can also see fires burning in the tropical rainforest.

f. There are other pine trees nearby, one of which is nearly 5,000 years old.

g. Over the years, various cartoonists gave him his characteristic appearance.

4 Here are seven questions, one for each text. What do the underlined words refer to?

1. Where is the oldest <u>one</u> in the world?
   tree
2. Why is <u>this</u> difficult to see from space?
3. Do <u>they</u> have the full range of emotions?
4. How did <u>they</u> become extinct?
5. What did <u>he</u> say "US" stood for?
6. Do <u>they</u> have a thirteenth floor?
7. Why are <u>they</u> more likely to have accidents?

Answer questions 1–7.

5 These numbers are from the texts. What do they refer to?

84	1815	1766	14	5,000
6	1906	200	83	15

Producing a class poster

6 What else would you like to know about the world? Work in groups and write some questions. Think of:

- places (countries, cities, buildings)
- people (customs, languages, superstitions, famous people)
- things (machines, gadgets, transportation, etc.)
- plants and animals

7 Choose two questions from Exercise 6 and research the answers. You could use the Internet, an encyclopedia, or other reference books from the library.

Make them into a poster for your classroom wall.

You ask ...

1

Q Do animals have feelings?

A All pet owners would say "Yes." Molly the dog and Whiskers the cat can feel angry, depressed, neglected, happy, even jealous and guilty.

Many scientists, however, are skeptical about giving animals the full range of emotions that humans can feel. Part of the problem is that it is impossible to prove that even a human being is feeling happy or sad. It is only because we can observe body language and facial expression that we can deduce it. And of course humans can express the emotion with language.

However, most researchers do agree that many creatures experience fear. Some scientists define this as a primary emotion. ____*d*____

2

Q What are the Earth's oldest living things?

A Trees! Two National Parks in California are home to our oldest living things. In the Giant Forest you'll find the largest sequoias /sɪˈkwɔɪyəz/ in the world, standing as tall as a 26-story building. Among them is a tree called General Sherman, which is 83 m tall and 31 m in circumference. This is the world's largest living thing. However, it isn't the oldest by any means. _____

3

Q What man-made things on Earth can be seen from space?

A "When humans first flew in space, they were amazed to discover that the only man-made object visible from orbit was the Great Wall of China." This is a nice idea, but it's not true. The Great Wall is mostly gray stone in a gray landscape and, in fact, is very difficult to see even from an airplane flying at a mere 15 kilometers above. What can be seen when orbiting the earth (from about 200 kilometers up) are the lights of the world's large metropolitan areas. _____

4

Q What is the most terrible natural disaster to have hit the Earth?

A Earthquakes, volcanic eruptions, and hurricanes are responsible for the deaths of thousands of people every year.

One of the most violent earthquakes ever recorded was in Ecuador in 1906. It was the equivalent of 100 H-bombs, but it was nothing compared to a volcanic eruption in Tambora, Indonesia in 1815. This was the equivalent of 10,000 H-bombs. But, even these are nothing compared to many tropical hurricanes: they regularly have the energy of an amazing 100,000 H-bombs.

However, there is one natural disaster that beats all of these by a very long way. A meteor that hit the Earth 65 million years ago and caused an explosion the equivalent of 10 million H-bombs. _____

5

Q Why isn't there a row 13 on airplanes?

A In many countries, the number 13 is considered to be very unlucky. In France, there is never a house with the number 13. In the United States, modern high-rise buildings label the floor that follows 12 as 14.

Where did this fear of a number come from? The idea goes back at least to Norse mythology in pre-Christian times. There was a banquet with 12 gods. Loki, the spirit of evil, decided to join without being invited. In the fight that followed, Balder, the favorite of the gods, was killed.

In Christianity, this theme was repeated at the Last Supper. Jesus Christ and his apostles numbered 13 people at the table. _____

6

Q Why do women live longer than men?

A Women generally live about 6 years longer than men. Evidence suggests that boys are the weaker sex at birth, which means that more die in infancy. Men also have a greater risk of heart disease than women, and they have heart attacks earlier in life. Men smoke and drink more than women, and their behavior is generally more aggressive, particularly when driving, so they are more likely to die in accidents. Also, men are more often in dangerous occupations, such as construction work.

Historically, women died in childbirth and men in wars. So nuns and philosophers often lived to great ages. Now childbearing is less risky and there are fewer wars. _____

7

Q Was Uncle Sam a real person?

A Yes, he was! This symbol of the United States with a long white beard, wearing striped pants and top hat, was a meat packer from New York state.

Uncle Sam was Samuel Wilson, born in Arlington, Massachusetts in 1766. At age eight, he was a drummer boy in the American Revolution. Later in life he moved to New York and opened a meat-packing company. He was a good and caring employer and became affectionately known as Uncle Sam.

Sam Wilson sold meat to the army, and he wrote the letters US on the crates. This meant "United States," but this abbreviation was not yet common. One day a company worker was asked what the letters US stood for. He wasn't sure, and said that perhaps the letters stood for his employer, Uncle Sam. This mistake continued. Soon soldiers started referring to all military goods as coming from Uncle Sam. They even saw themselves as Uncle Sam's men. _____

VOCABULARY AND IDIOMS
What can your body do?

1 As a class, write all the parts of the body that you know on the board.

2 Work in pairs. Say which parts of the body you use to do these things.

kick	bite	hit	hold	hug	kiss	lick	point
climb	think	chew	whistle	stare	drop	

3 Which verbs go with which nouns and phrases? Match a word in **A** with a line in **B**.

A	B	A	B
whistle	a ladder	kiss	into an apple
lick	litter on the ground	point	me on the cheek
climb	into the distance	hit	about the meaning of life
drop	a tune	think	a soccer ball
hug	your grandmother	bite	a gun
stare	gum	kick	a nail with a hammer
chew	an ice-cream cone	hold	me in your arms

4 Look at these idioms formed with some of the verbs. Can you guess their meaning?

hold your breath	kick the habit	think twice (about something)
kiss something good-bye	hit the roof	drop someone a line

Fill in the blanks with the idioms above. If necessary, change the form of the verb. The first letter of each missing word is given.

1. The best way to stop hiccups is to h_____ your b_____ and count to ten.
2. My parents h_____ the r_____ when I said I'd been to an all-night party.
3. I've tried so many times to stop biting my nails, but I just can't k_____ the h_____ .
4. I almost bought a new sports car, but then I t_____ t_____ about it and realized it wasn't such a great idea.
5. **A** I lost my purse with $200 in it.
   B Well, you can k_____ that money g_____ !
6. D_____ me a l_____ when you know what time you're coming, and I'll meet you at the station.

LISTENING AND SPEAKING
The forgetful generation

1 **T 11.8** Listen to the introduction to a radio program called "What's Your Problem?" and answer the questions.
   1. What problem are they talking about?
   2. What do they think is causing it?

2 Discuss these questions.
   • Does your lifestyle mean that you have a lot to remember to do each day?
   • Do you think modern society is busier and more stressful than 100 years ago?
   • How do you remember all the things that you have to do each day?

3 **T 11.9** Listen to the stories of LeeAnn, Jerry, and Keiko, and take notes about them in the chart.

What did they forget?	What did they do?
LeeAnn	
Jerry	
Keiko	

4 **T 11.10** Listen to the rest of the radio program and answer the questions.

1. What is Professor Alan Buchan's job?
2. What is it about some modern day working practices that causes forgetfulness?
3. Why did the lady think that she was going insane?
4. What was the lady's problem?
5. What helped the lady feel more relaxed?
6. Does Professor Buchan advise using a personal computer to help remember things?
7. What does he advise? Why does he advise this?
8. How does the presenter try to be funny at the end of the interview?

What do you think?

Do you think Professor Buchan's explanation for forgetfulness is true? Do you know any stories of forgetfulness, either your own or somebody else's?

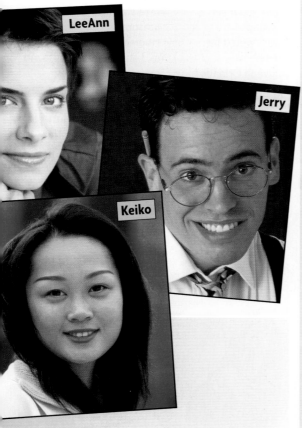

LeeAnn

Jerry

Keiko

WRITING: For and against
▶▶ Go to page 120

EVERYDAY ENGLISH
Informal English

1 When we speak, we use a lot of informal language, depending on who we're speaking to!

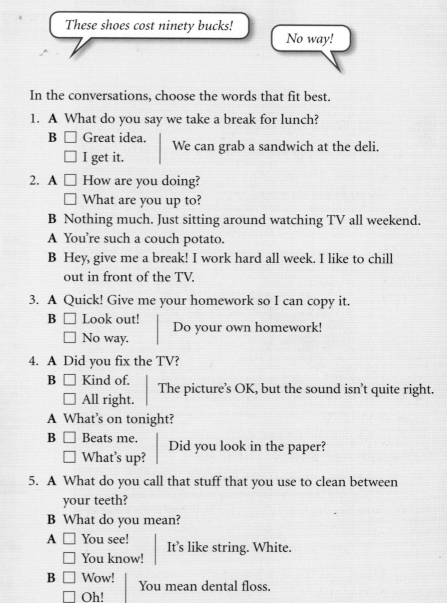

These shoes cost ninety bucks!

No way!

In the conversations, choose the words that fit best.

1. **A** What do you say we take a break for lunch?
   B ☐ Great idea.
      ☐ I get it. │ We can grab a sandwich at the deli.

2. **A** ☐ How are you doing?
      ☐ What are you up to?
   B Nothing much. Just sitting around watching TV all weekend.
   A You're such a couch potato.
   B Hey, give me a break! I work hard all week. I like to chill out in front of the TV.

3. **A** Quick! Give me your homework so I can copy it.
   B ☐ Look out! │ Do your own homework!
      ☐ No way.

4. **A** Did you fix the TV?
   B ☐ Kind of. │ The picture's OK, but the sound isn't quite right.
      ☐ All right.
   A What's on tonight?
   B ☐ Beats me. │ Did you look in the paper?
      ☐ What's up?

5. **A** What do you call that stuff that you use to clean between your teeth?
   B What do you mean?
   A ☐ You see! │ It's like string. White.
      ☐ You know!
   B ☐ Wow! │ You mean dental floss.
      ☐ Oh!
   A Yeah. That's it!

T 11.11 Listen and check. Practice the conversations with a partner.

2 There are lots of other examples of informal language in the conversations. How do we say them more formally? Be careful if you try to use them!

12 Life's great events!

Reported speech • Reporting verbs • Birth, marriage, and death • Saying sorry

TEST YOUR GRAMMAR

1 Read the story of Joel and Tara in **A** and complete their actual conversation in **B**.

THE MARRIAGE PROPOSAL

A Joel greeted Tara and asked how she was.

She told him she was fine.

He said it was great to see her again.

She said they hadn't seen each other for a while.

Joel said there was something he wanted to ask her. He told Tara that he loved her and asked if she would marry him.

She said that she would and that she loved him too.

B Joel "Hi, Tara. How <u>are you</u> ?"

Tara "I'm _____ , thanks."

Joel "It's _____ to see you again."

Tara "You too. We _____ seen each other for a while."

Joel "Yes. You know, there _____ something I _____ to ask you. ... I _____ you. _____ you _____ me?"

Tara "Oh, yes! Yes, I _____ . I _____ you, too."

2 Which is direct speech and which is reported speech?

THE WEDDING
Reported statements and questions

1 Elliot and Martha are guests at Joel and Tara's wedding in Atlanta. Match a line in **A** with a line in **B** to complete their conversation.

A	Elliot	B	Martha
1.	How do you know Joel and Tara?		Yes, we do.
2.	Are you married?		Sure. I'll introduce you to my husband.
3.	Where did you meet your husband?		We're staying at the Four Seasons Hotel.
4.	Have you traveled far to get here?		I studied at UCLA with Tara.
5.	Do you live in Orlando?		Yes, I am. That's my husband over there.
6.	So, where are you staying in Atlanta?		Actually, I met him at a wedding.
7.	So am I. Can we meet there later for coffee?		No, we haven't. We just got here yesterday. We flew in from Orlando.

2 **T 12.1** Listen and check.

3 Martha is telling her husband, Ron, about the conversation with Elliot. Read what she says.

"I just met this really nice guy named Elliot. He was very friendly. Do you know what he said? First, he asked me how I **knew** *Joel and Tara. I told him that I* **had studied** *with Tara at UCLA. Then he asked if I* **was** *married. Of course I said that I* **was**! *And next …"*

GRAMMAR SPOT

1 Complete the reported speech.

Direct speech	Reported speech
"**Are** you married?" he asked.	He asked if I <u>was</u> married.
"We**'re** married," she said.	She said that they <u>were</u> married.
"How **do** you **know** Joel and Tara?" he asked.	He asked me how I _____ Joel and Tara.
"I **studied** with Tara," she told him.	She told him that she _____ with Tara.

2 What happens to tenses in reported speech?

3 What is the difference in the way *say* and *tell* are used?

4 When is *if* used?

▶▶ **Grammar Reference 12.1–12.3 p. 151**

PRACTICE

What did Elliot say?

1 Continue reporting Martha's conversation with Elliot. Work with a partner.

"… *next he asked where we'd met and I told him that we …"*

2 **T 12.2** Listen to Martha reporting the conversation to her husband.

He's a liar!

3 Martha and Ron are talking about Elliot. Complete Martha's lines in the conversation.

1. **R** Elliot lives in Detroit.
   M But he told me he <u>lived in New York.</u> (New York)
2. **R** He doesn't like his new job.
   M But he said that he _____ it! (love)
3. **R** He's moving to Iowa.
   M But he told me _____ ! (Florida)
4. **R** He stayed home on his last vacation.
   M But he told me _____ ! (Paris)
5. **R** He'll be 40 next week.
   M But he told me _____ ! (30)
6. **R** He's been married three times.
   M But he told me _____ ! (never/married)
   R You see! I told you he was a liar!

4 **T 12.3** Listen and check. Pay particular attention to the stress and intonation. Practice the conversation with a partner.

Discussing grammar

5 Work with a partner. What's the difference in meaning in the following pairs of sentences? When does *'d = had*? When does *'d = would*?

1. He asked them how they'd traveled to Acapulco.
   He asked them how they'd travel to Acapulco.
2. She told her mother that she loved Joel.
   She told her mother that she'd love Joel.
3. She said they lived in Orlando.
   She said they'd lived in Orlando.

What did the people actually say in direct speech?

6 Change the direct speech into reported speech.

1. "I'm tired!" he said. **He said that he was tired.**
2. "Are you leaving on Friday?" she asked me.
3. "We haven't seen Jack for a long time," they said.
4. "We flew to Tokyo," they said.
5. "Which airport did you fly from?" I asked them.
6. "The flight has been canceled," the announcement said.
7. "I'll call you later," he said.
8. "We can't do the exercise," they told the teacher.

GO TO JAIL!
Reported commands and requests

1 Read the newspaper article. Name the people in the photos.

"A Marriage Made in Hell!"

This is how Judge Margaret Kramer described the marriage of Kenny and Kathleen Brady as she ordered them to spend 14 days in jail.

THE COUPLE married only six months ago, and already they are famous for their fights. Neighbors complained that they could hear them shouting from across the street. Ann West, who lives next door, said, "First I asked them nicely to stop because my baby couldn't get to sleep, but they didn't. Then my husband knocked on their door and told them to stop, but they refused to listen. They threw a chair out the window at him. It just missed him! So that was it! We called the police and asked them to come right away."

Mr. and Mrs. Brady admitted they had been arguing. Mrs. Brady said that she had accused Mr. Brady of wasting their money on drinking and gambling. However, they denied throwing the chair.

The judge clearly did not believe them. She reminded them that they had already had two previous warnings from the police. She advised them to talk to a marriage counselor after they'd served 14 days in jail.

Mr. and Mrs. West and their baby are looking forward to some sleep!

2 Who is speaking? Find the lines in the text that report the following sentences.

1. "You have to go to jail for 14 days."
   Judge Kramer ordered them to spend 14 days in jail.
2. "It's terrible. We can hear them shouting from across the street."
3. "Please, will you stop making noise? My baby can't get to sleep."
4. "Stop making that noise!"
5. "Please, can you come right away?"
6. "OK. OK. It's true. We were arguing."
7. "You've been wasting our money on drinking and gambling again!"
8. "We didn't throw the chair."
9. "Remember that you have already had two warnings from the police."
10. "I think you should see a marriage counselor after you've served 14 days in jail."

GRAMMAR SPOT

1 Which sentence is a reported statement? Which is a reported command?
   He **told them to stop** making noise.
   He **told them that she lived** on the next block.

2 Which sentence is a reported question? Which is a reported request?
   I **asked them to stop** making noise.
   She **asked me if I had met** them before.

3 *Say, tell,* and *ask* are all used in reported speech. Underline other verbs in the article that can be used to report conversations. *She ordered them.*

▶▶ **Grammar Reference 12.4 p. 151**

PRACTICE

Other reporting verbs

1 Match the verbs with the direct speech.

a. ask   e. remind
b. tell   f. advise
c. order   g. beg
d. invite   h. refuse

1. "Sign on the dotted line," the mail carrier said to me. __*b*__
2. "Please, can you translate this sentence for me?" Maria said to Mark. _____
3. "Don't forget to send Aunt Judy a birthday card," Mary said to her son. _____
4. "Please, please, please marry me. I can't live without you," Joel said to Tara. _____
5. "Please come to our wedding," Joel said to his boss. _____
6. "I won't go to bed!" Tommy said. _____
7. "You should talk to your lawyer," Ben said to Bill. _____
8. "Take that gum out of your mouth right now!" the teacher said to Joanna. _____

2 Put the sentences in Exercise 1 into reported speech using the verbs 1–8.

The mail carrier told me to sign on the dotted line.

T 12.4 Listen and check.

Listening and note-taking

1 You are police officers taking statements. Divide into two groups.

T 12.5 Group A Listen to Kathleen Brady and take notes.

T 12.6 Group B Listen to Ann West and take notes.

2 Find a partner from the other group and report what you heard. Find the differences. Begin like this.

A Kathleen admitted that they sometimes argued. She said that ...

B Ann complained that they argued every night. She said that ...

3 Write the reports for the police records. You can use the verbs below.

admit apologize complain offer order promise refuse say tell

There is a list of verb patterns on page 153.

VOCABULARY AND SPEAKING
Birth, marriage, and death

1 Use your dictionary to sort the following words and phrases into the categories in the chart.

> wedding funeral get engaged have a baby bouquet
> wreath pregnant reception bury groom midwife widow
> crib mourners honeymoon diaper get divorced coffin

BIRTH	MARRIAGE	DEATH
have a baby		

2 Here are the opening and closing lines of a short story of a long life.

> VICTOR PARROT was born one cold, stormy night in ...

> He died, aged ninety-five, with a smile on his face. Over five hundred mourners came to his funeral ...

Work with a partner. Write the story of the main events of Victor's life. Use as many of the words from Exercise 1 as possible. Read your story aloud to the class.

3 What happens at births, weddings, and funerals in your country?

LISTENING AND SPEAKING
A birth

1 Work in small groups.

Obviously you can't remember anything about the day you were born, but what have you been told about it? Who told you? What did they say?

Tell any interesting stories to the whole class.

2 **T 12.7** Lenora Switt's family comes from Prince Edward Island, Canada. Listen to her telling the story of her Great Aunt Dodi's birth and complete the sentences.

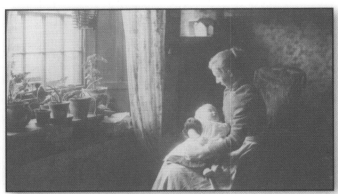

1. My aunt was born on Prince Edward Island on January ___16___ , _____ .
2. She was the _____ of _____ children.
3. The _____ only just managed to get there in time.
4. She said, "I'm afraid the child isn't _____ ."
5. My great-grandmother _____ the baby and ran downstairs.
6. She opened the door of the wood stove and put the _____ into the oven.
7. A few minutes later, a great _____ _____ came from the oven.
8. My Great Aunt Dodi is still _____ . She has _____ grandchildren and _____ great-grandchildren.

Role play

3 Work with a partner.

Student A Imagine you are Great Aunt Dodi. Tell the story of your birth to one of your grandchildren.
Student B You are one of Great Aunt Dodi's grandchildren. She is telling you again the story of her birth. Remind her that you've heard it many times before.

A Have I ever told you the story of when I was born? It was January ...
B Yes, I know, and it was very cold ...

READING AND SPEAKING
A death

1 You are going to read and listen to a poem by W.H. Auden (1907–1973). The poem is called "Funeral Blues." What does the title tell you about the poem?

2 **T 12.8** Close your books and close your eyes and listen to the poem. Don't try to understand every word.
1. What has happened?
2. How does the writer feel about the world now?
3. What words or lines can you remember?

Share what you can remember with the rest of the class.

3 Read the poem and answer the questions. Use your dictionary to check new words.
1. A loved one has died. What, in general, does the poet want the rest of the world to do? Why does the poet feel like this?
2. Which lines describe things that could possibly happen? Which lines describe impossible things?
3. Which verse describes the closeness of the relationship?
4. When you fall in love it is said that you see the world through "rose-colored glasses." What does this mean? In what ways is the poem the opposite of this?

Learning by heart

4 Divide into four groups.
1. Each group should choose one verse and learn it by heart.
2. Recite the poem around the class.

FUNERAL BLUES

Stop all the clocks, cut off the telephone,
Prevent the dog from barking with a juicy bone,
Silence the pianos and with muffled drum
Bring out the coffin, let the mourners come.

Let airplanes circle moaning overhead
Scribbling on the sky the message *He Is Dead*,
Put crepe bows round the white necks of the public doves,
Let the traffic policemen wear black cotton gloves.

He was my North, my South, my East and West,
My working week and my Sunday rest,
My noon, my midnight, my talk, my song;
I thought that love would last forever: I was wrong.

The stars are not wanted now; put out every one;
Pack up the moon and dismantle the sun;
Pour away the ocean and sweep up the wood;
For nothing now can ever come to any good.

W. H. Auden (1907–1973)

LISTENING AND SPEAKING
My Way

1 **T 12.9** Listen to the song called "My Way" made famous by Frank Sinatra.
- What is the message about life in this song?
- At what stage in his life is the singer?

2 Work with a partner. Discuss which words on the right best complete the lines.

Frank Sinatra

3 **T 12.9** Listen again and check. Sing along if you can!

WRITING: Correcting mistakes
▶▶ Go to page 121

My Way

And now, the end is near
And so I ___(1)___ the final curtain
My friend, I'll say it clear
I'll ___(2)___ my case, of which I'm certain
I've lived a life that's full
I've ___(3)___ each and every highway
And more, much more than this,
I did it my way ...

Regrets, I've had ___(4)___
But then again, too few to mention
I did what I ___(5)___ to do
and saw it through without exemption,
I planned each charted course,
each careful ___(6)___ along the byway
And more, much more than this,
I did it my way ...

Yes, there were ___(7)___,
I'm sure you knew,
When I bit off
more than I could ___(8)___
But through it all,
when there was doubt
I ate it up and spit it out
I faced it all and I stood ___(9)___
and did it my way ...

I've loved, I've ___(10)___ and cried
I've had my fill, my share of losing
And now, as tears subside,
I find it all so ___(11)___
To think I did all that
And may I say, not in a ___(12)___ way,
"Oh, no, oh, no, not me, I did it my way."
For what is a man, what has he got?
If not himself, then he has ___(13)___.
To say the things he truly ___(14)___
and not the words of one who kneels,
The record shows I took the ___(15)___
and did it my way ...
Yes, it was my way ...

1.	meet	face
2.	state	say
3.	traveled	ridden
4.	a lot	a few
5.	had	wanted
6.	step	stop
7.	days	times
8.	chew	eat
9.	tall	up
10.	joked	laughed
11.	exciting	amusing
12.	sad	shy
13.	nothing	naught
14.	feels	knows
15.	blows	time

EVERYDAY ENGLISH
Saying sorry

1 Read the conversations and fill in the blanks with the correct expressions from the box.

(I'm) sorry   I'm so sorry   Pardon me   Excuse me   What

1. **A** _____ , what's that creature called?
   B It's a Tyrannosaurus.
   A _____ ?
   B A Tyrannosaurus. Tyrannosaurus Rex.
   A Thank you very much.

2. **A** Ouch! That's my foot!
   B _____ . I wasn't looking where I was going.

3. **A** Excuse me, can you tell me where the post office is?
   B _____ , I'm a stranger here myself.

4. **A** I failed my driving test for the sixth time!
   B _____ .

5. **A** _____ ! We need to get past. My little boy isn't feeling well.

6. **A** Do you want your hearing aid, Grandma?
   B _____ ?
   A I said: Do you want your hearing aid?
   B _____ ?
   A DO YOU WANT YOUR HEARING AID?!
   B _____ , I can't hear you. I need my hearing aid.

2 **T 12.10** Listen and check. Practice the conversations with a partner.

3 What exactly would you say in the following situations?
Use about two to four sentences in your response.

1. You were cut off in the middle of an important phone call to a business colleague. You call your colleague back.

2. You want the attention of the waiter in a very crowded restaurant. You want another large bottle of mineral water for your table.

3. A friend tells you that she can't meet you for lunch as planned next Thursday because she suddenly has to go to an aunt's funeral.

4. You thought you had bought a medium-size sweater, but when you get home you see it is the wrong size. You take it back to the store.

5. You want to get off a very crowded train at the next stop. You have a large suitcase.

6. Your dinner guest reminds you that he is a vegetarian. You have just put a huge steak on his plate.

> Hello? I think we must have been cut off. I'm sorry about that.

This page has been left blank.

Pages 98–102 (the Getting Information pages for Units 1–6)
appear in Student Book 3A.

Getting Information

UNIT 7, page 55

READING AND SPEAKING
Role play

1 Work with a partner.

Student A Imagine that you are a journalist. Interview your partner about his/her dream job from Exercise 1 on page 54. Ask these questions.

- What do you do?
- How did you get the job?
- What do you like most about it?
- What's an average day like?
- Have you made any sacrifices to do this job?
- What would you like to do next?
- What advice would you give to someone who wanted to do your job?

Student B Imagine that you actually do your dream job from Exercise 1 on page 54. Your partner is a journalist. Answer his/her questions.

2 Switch roles.

Student A Imagine that you actually do your dream job.

Student B Imagine that you are a journalist. Interview Student A.

I NEED HELP!
Lucy and Pam's letters

Here are Lucy and Pam's letters to "Debbie's Problem Page."

Dear Debbie,

I am 16 years old and totally depressed. I'm in love with Leon Rossi, the movie star. I think of him night and day. I just sit in my room and watch videos of his movies over and over. I've written hundreds of letters to him and sent e-mails to his fan club, but all I get back are autographed photos. I dream that someday I'll meet him and that he'll feel the same way about me. My friends think I'm crazy, so I don't see them anymore. I can't concentrate on my homework, and I have final exams next month. I've tried to talk to my Mom and Dad, but they're both lawyers and much too busy to listen to me.

Please, please help me! I'm desperate. I'm thinking of running away to Hollywood to meet him.

Yours in misery,

Lucy

Dear Debbie,

I'm almost too tired to write, but I have no one to turn to. I've been married for three years and everything was just fine until a year ago when Brian, my husband, lost his job. He became depressed, and because he has nothing to do, he just goes over to his mother's house on the next block and spends all day with her. He says he's worried about her because she lives alone.

I'm a nurse at a hospital. I'm exhausted after work, but when I get home I have to cook and clean the house. Brian refuses to cook or do housework—he says it's boring and gets angry with me if I ask him to do anything around the house. His whole personality has changed—we just don't communicate anymore. Also, I'm worried that he's becoming a problem gambler. I found hundreds of lottery tickets in a drawer yesterday, but I haven't said anything about it.

What can I do? I still love him. We were hoping to start a family soon, but now I'm not so sure this is a good idea.

Sincerely,

Pam

PRACTICE

Who's who in the family?

1 Work in small groups. Look at the photos. They are all of Jeff and his family. In each photo, which one do you think is Jeff?

Who do you think the others are?
Why?

2 Check your guesses. Go to page 109.

> *This must be Jeff because …*

> *But this could be Jeff …*

PRACTICE

Information gap

Ask and answer questions to complete the information about Walt Disney. Write in the replies your partner gives you.

Student A When was Walt Disney born?
Student B On December 5, 1901.
              Where did he live?
Student A On his parents' farm in Missouri.
              What jobs … ?

WALT DISNEY

Walt Disney was born _on December 5, 1901_ (When?), and lived on his parents' farm in Missouri. His family was poor and Walt had a difficult childhood. He had to work many different jobs to earn extra money—_____ (What jobs?). He became interested in drawing when he was about seven, but his father thought it was a waste of time.

The Disney family moved to _____ (Where to?) when Walt was 12. He started going to art classes where he learned to draw cartoons. Then the United States entered World War I in _____ (When?). Walt was only 16, but he forged his parents' signatures and went to France to become an ambulance driver for the Red Cross. His ambulance was covered with _____ (What?).

After the war, Walt worked as a commercial artist. He produced a series of short films called _____ (What called?). He was paid $1,500 for each film. This was his first break. Walt met and married one of his employees, _____ (Who?), when he was 24, and the marriage lasted until his death 41 years later.

One of Walt's early creations was Mickey Mouse, and Walt provided Mickey's voice. Mickey's first animated movie was called _____ (What?), which came out in 1928. It was a huge success. He went on to win _____ (How many?) Academy Awards® for his animated movies, and in 1955 he opened the first Disneyland park in _____ (Where?). He died in 1966.

PRACTICE

Conversations

1 Work with a partner. Choose one of the conversations below and add
question tags.

Conversation 1

A You broke that vase.
B Yes, I did. I dropped it. I'm sorry.
A You'll replace it.
B Yes, of course I will. How much did it cost?
A $300.
B $300?! It *wasn't* that much.
A Yes, it *was*.

Conversation 2

A Did you pay the electric bill?
B No, *you* paid it.
A No, I didn't pay it. I thought you paid it.
B Me? You *always* pay it.
A No, I don't. I always pay the phone bill.
B Oh, that's right.

Conversation 3

A We love each other.
B Um, I think so.
A We don't ever want to be apart.
B Well …
A And we'll get married and have lots of children.
B What? You didn't buy me a ring.
A Yes, I did. Diamonds are forever.
B Oh, no!

Conversation 4

A Helen didn't win the lottery.
B Yes, she did. She won $4 million!
A She isn't going to give it all to charity.
B As a matter of fact, she is.
A Wow. Not many people would do that.
B Well, *I* certainly wouldn't.

Conversation 5

A I think we're lost. Let's look at the map.
B Uh-oh.
A What do you mean, "Uh-oh"? You didn't forget the map?
B Sorry.
A How are we going to get back to the campground without a map?
B Well, we could ask a police officer.
A There aren't many police officers on this mountain!

2 Act out your conversation for the class.

PRACTICE
Information gap

Ask and answer questions to complete the information about Walt Disney. Write in the replies your partner gives you.

Student A When was Walt Disney born?
Student B On December 5, 1901.
Where did he live?
Student A On his parents' farm in Missouri.
What jobs … ?

WALT DISNEY

Walt Disney was born on December 5, 1901, and lived <u>on his parents' farm</u> *(Where?)* in Missouri. His family was poor and Walt had a difficult childhood. He had to work many different jobs to earn extra money—delivering papers, picking apples, and helping on the farm. He became interested in drawing when he was _____ *(How old?)*, but his father thought it was a waste of time.

The Disney family moved to Chicago when Walt was 12. He started going to art classes where he learned to _____ *(What?)*. Then the United States entered World War I in 1917. Walt was only 16, but he forged his parents' signatures and went to France to _____ *(Why?)*. His ambulance was covered with Disney cartoons.

After the war, Walt worked as a _____ *(What?)*. He produced a series of short films called *Alice in Cartoonland*. He was paid _____ *(How much?)* for each film. This was his first break. Walt met and married one of his employees, Lillian Bounds, when he was 24, and the marriage lasted _____ *(How long?)*.

One of Walt's early creations was Mickey Mouse, and Walt provided Mickey's voice. Mickey's first animated movie was called *Steamboat Willie*, which came out _____ *(When?)*. It was a huge success. He went on to win 32 Academy Awards® for his animated movies, and in _____ *(When?)* he opened the first Disneyland park in Anaheim, California. He died in 1966.

PRACTICE
Who's who in the family?

Picture 1 *(back row, left to right)* grandmother, grandfather
                (front row, left to right) brother, Jeff

Picture 2 *(left to right)* father, wife, Jeff, mother, brother

Picture 3 *(back row, left to right)* Jeff, wife, mother, brother, sister-in-law
                (middle row, left to right) son, niece, niece
                (front row, left to right) son, nephew

Picture 4 *(left to right)* son, Jeff, daughter, son, wife

Writing

WRITING
Writing a cover letter

1 Complete Heather Mann's cover letter to Worldwatch Americas with the words from the box.

> qualifications advertisement
> studied to interested fluent
> traveled for have

2 Write a cover letter for the following job advertisement.

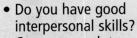

TRANS-GLOBE TOURS

Tour Guides

Europe –
East Asia –
South America

- Do you have good interpersonal skills?
- Can you speak two or more languages?
- Do you want to see the world?

Please apply with resume to:
Human Resources
Trans-Globe Tours
144 E. 42nd Street
New York, NY 10017

HEATHER W. MANN
3421 Irish Road • Berwyn, PA 19312 • (610) 555-3762

January 17, 2003

George Butler
Worldwatch Americas
7950 Merritts Avenue
Overland Park, IL 51551

Dear Mr. Butler:

I saw your <u>advertisement</u> for a Business Journalist in today's *Chicago Tribune*. I am very _____ in the job and I think that I have many of the necessary _____ .

I _____ journalism and modern languages at Boston University. I am _____ in Spanish and Portuguese. I have _____ widely in Europe and South America, and I _____ worked as a journalist for Intertec Publishing _____ the last five years.

Enclosed is a copy of my resume. I look forward _____ hearing from you soon. Please let me know if you need more information.

Sincerely,

Heather Mann

Heather Mann

WRITING
Words that join ideas

! **1** Some words and expressions are used to make a comment on what is being expressed.

In fact = I'm going to give you some more detailed information.
Peter doesn't like carrots. **In fact,** he hates them!

Of course = I'm going to tell you something you expect to hear.
Of course, having a baby has changed our life a lot.

Actually = I'm going to give you some information you didn't know.
Actually, Jane knows a lot about food. Her parents own a restaurant.

Unfortunately = I'm going to give you some news that is bad.
Unfortunately, there was nothing we could do to help.

Nevertheless = The result or effect of something is not what you would expect.
The accident wasn't her fault. **Nevertheless,** she felt bad.

Anyway = Let's change the subject and talk about something else.
What an awful trip you had! You must be exhausted!
Anyway, you're here now so let's not worry anymore.

2 Some words are used to join ideas and sentences.

George was rich. He wasn't a happy man.
Although George was rich, he wasn't a happy man.
George was rich. **However,** he wasn't a happy man.
George was rich, **but** he wasn't a happy man.

Carol called me. She couldn't find her passport.
Carol called me **because** she couldn't find her passport.
Carol couldn't find her passport, **so** she called me.

Read the e-mail and write the word or words that fit best.

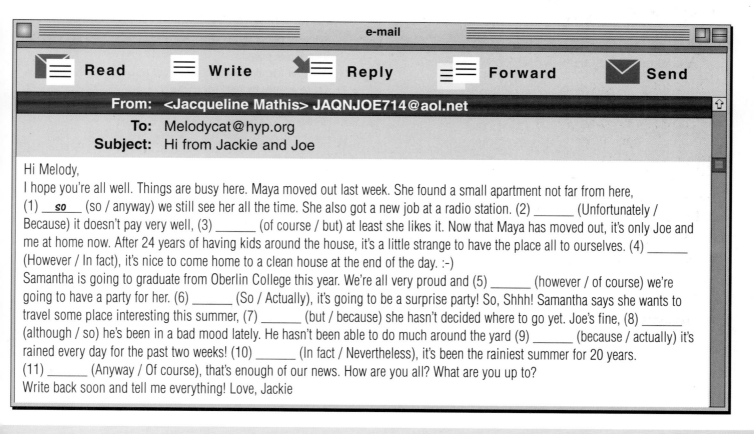

e-mail

Read   **Write**   **Reply**   **Forward**   **Send**

From: \<Jacqueline Mathis> JAQNJOE714@aol.net
To: Melodycat@hyp.org
Subject: Hi from Jackie and Joe

Hi Melody,
I hope you're all well. Things are busy here. Maya moved out last week. She found a small apartment not far from here,
(1) __so__ (so / anyway) we still see her all the time. She also got a new job at a radio station. (2) _____ (Unfortunately / Because) it doesn't pay very well, (3) _____ (of course / but) at least she likes it. Now that Maya has moved out, it's only Joe and me at home now. After 24 years of having kids around the house, it's a little strange to have the place all to ourselves. (4) _____ (However / In fact), it's nice to come home to a clean house at the end of the day. :-)
Samantha is going to graduate from Oberlin College this year. We're all very proud and (5) _____ (however / of course) we're going to have a party for her. (6) _____ (So / Actually), it's going to be a surprise party! So, Shhh! Samantha says she wants to travel some place interesting this summer, (7) _____ (but / because) she hasn't decided where to go yet. Joe's fine, (8) _____ (although / so) he's been in a bad mood lately. He hasn't been able to do much around the yard (9) _____ (because / actually) it's rained every day for the past two weeks! (10) _____ (In fact / Nevertheless), it's been the rainiest summer for 20 years.
(11) _____ (Anyway / Of course), that's enough of our news. How are you all? What are you up to?
Write back soon and tell me everything! Love, Jackie

WRITING
Beginning and ending letters

> ⓘ Notice the following points about formal and informal letters:
>
> 1 We can write contractions *(I've, we've, I'll)* in an informal letter, but not in a formal one.
>
> All letters begin with *Dear,*
> You can end an informal letter with *Best wishes* or *Love.*
>
> 2 Here are some useful phrases for informal letters:
> **Beginning**
> • It was great to hear from you. I was happy to hear that ...
> • Thank you for your letter. I was sorry to hear that ...
> • I'm sorry I haven't written before, but ...
> • This is just a note to say ...
> **Ending**
> • I'm looking forward to seeing you ...
> • I'm looking forward to hearing from you soon ...
> • Say hello to Robert ...
> • Write to me soon ...
> • I hope to hear from you soon ...
> • Write and tell me when ...

1 Look at the chart below and match the beginning of each letter to the sentence that follows it. Which letter ...

- asks for information?
- accepts an invitation?
- invites people?
- says that money has been received?
- gives news?

2 Match each ending to one of the letters in Exercise 1.

_3_ Thank you very much. I look forward to hearing from you in the near future.
Sincerely,
James Fox

_____ We will complete your order as soon as we can.
Sincerely,
Silicon Valley Software

_____ It would be great to meet sometime. Please let me know if you ever come to Boston.
Love,
Pat

_____ Write back soon and tell me if you can make it.
Yours,
Peter

_____ We're really looking forward to seeing you again and meeting your friends.
Best wishes,
Mary

3 Write a letter to a friend who you haven't been in touch with for a long time. Include the following parts:

- Tell your friend about what you've been doing recently. Include your future plans.
- Ask your friend about his/her recent activities and future plans.
- Try to arrange to meet somewhere.
- Remember to put your address and the date in the top right-hand corner of your letter.

A	B
1. Dear Mary, This is just a note to ask if you and Dave are free on the evening of July 11.	Could you please send me your brochure and a price list?
2. Dear Jane, Thanks for your letter. It was good to hear from you after such a long time. You asked me what I've been doing. Well, ...	I've changed jobs a few times since I last spoke to you and, as you know, I've moved, too.
3. Dear Sir or Madam, I saw an advertisement in *The Chicago Tribune* for weekend specials at your hotel.	Unfortunately, this amount did not include shipping and handling, which is $7.50.
4. Dear Peter, Thank you so much for inviting Dave and me to your summer party.	Jen and I are having a barbecue with all our friends, and we were wondering if you could come.
5. Dear Mr. Smith, We received your order for the *World Encyclopedia* on CD-ROM, and your check for $75.	We'd love to come. I haven't been to your place for a long time.

WRITING
Sentence combination

1 Read the sentences about Johnny Appleseed and then compare them with the paragraph below. Notice the ways that the sentences are combined.

Johnny Appleseed's real name was John Chapman.
He was born in 1774.
He was born in Massachusetts.
He traveled westward.
At that time, he was 23 years old.
He went to the Ohio River Valley.
He found no apple orchards.
He found no apple trees.
Johnny had a love of nature.
This love gave him an idea.
He planted thousands of seeds.
The seeds were for apples.
The seeds grew into apple trees.
This made the wilderness bloom.
Johnny Appleseed died in 1845.
He spent 50 years traveling and planting seeds.
Some of the trees still bear apples.
He planted those trees 200 years ago.

Johnny Appleseed, whose real name was John Chapman, was born in Massachusetts in 1774. When he was 23 years old, he traveled westward to the Ohio River Valley, where he found no apple orchards or apple trees. Johnny's love of nature gave him an idea. He planted thousands of apple seeds, which grew into apple trees, making the wilderness bloom. Johnny Appleseed died in 1845, after 50 years of traveling and planting seeds. Some of the trees that he planted 200 years ago still bear apples.

2 Rewrite each group of sentences to form a more natural sounding paragraph.
1. **A person**

Alicia Vargas is a writer.
She writes mysteries.
She is famous.
She comes from Chile.
She has recently moved to California.
She has written 25 novels.
Her novels have been translated into 15 languages.
A Hollywood studio is going to make a movie of her latest novel.
The novel is called *A Charmed Life*.
The movie will star Sunny Shaw.
Sunny Shaw's last movie was a huge box-office success.
The movie was called *Hot Night in the Snow*.

2. **A place**

Philadelphia was founded in 1682.
It was founded by William Penn.
It is the largest city in the state of Pennsylvania.
It is the fifth largest city in the United States.
Its name comes from the Greek.
In Greek, it means "city of brotherly love."
Philadelphia is sometimes called the birthplace of the nation.
It is where the Declaration of Independence was signed in 1776.
It is where the Constitution was signed in 1787.
Philadelphia was the capital of the United States from 1790 to 1800.
Not everyone knows this.
Philadelphia is also the home of the Liberty Bell.
The Liberty Bell is famous.
It weighs 909 kilograms.
It is now kept in a special glass pavilion for visitors to view.

3 Write a short profile of a person or a place that is important to you.

WRITING
For and against

1 Do you live or work in a city? Is it very big? Write down five advantages and five disadvantages of living in the city. Compare your ideas with a partner.

2 Write down five advantages and five disadvantages of living in the country. Compare your ideas with your partner.

3 Read the text and add the phrases from the box.

> finally   all in all   one disadvantage is that   especially
> has both advantages and disadvantages   for example
> what's more   in conclusion   one advantage is that

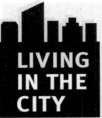

LIVING IN THE CITY

Living in the city (1) __has both advantages and disadvantages__ . (2) _____ it is often easier to find work, and there is usually good public transportation, so you don't need to own a car. Also, there are a lot of interesting things to do and places to see. (3) _____ , you can eat in good restaurants, visit museums, and go to the theater and to concerts. (4) _____ , when you want to relax, you can usually find a park where you can feed the ducks or just sit on a park bench and read a book. (5) _____ , city life is full of bustle and variety and you need never feel bored.

However, for every plus there is a minus. (6) _____ , you might have a job, but unless it pays very well, you will not be able to afford many of the things that there are to do, because living in a city is often very expensive. It is (7) _____ difficult to find good, cheap housing. What's more, public transportation is sometimes crowded and dirty, particularly during rush hour. Even the parks can become very crowded, especially on Sundays when it seems as if everyone is looking for some open space and green grass. (8) _____ , despite all the crowds, it is still possible to feel lonely in a city.

(9) _____ , I think that city life can be particularly appealing to young people, who like the excitement of the city and don't mind the noise and pollution. However, many people, when they get older, and particularly when they have young children, often prefer the peace and fresh air of the suburbs.

4 There are three paragraphs. What is the purpose of each one?

5 Write three paragraphs entitled "Living in the Country" about the advantages and disadvantages of living in the country. In the conclusion, give your own opinion. Write about 250 words.

WRITING
Correcting mistakes

1 Ana was a student of English in Chicago, where she stayed with the Bennett family. She has now returned home. Read the letter she has written to Mr. and Mrs. Bennett. Her English has improved, but there are still over 25 mistakes. How many can you find?

28 Nuevo Leon
Mexico City
Mexico, D.F.

Friday, June 14

Dear Mr. and Mrs. Bennett,

I am home now since two weeks, but I have to start work immediately, so this is the first time is possible for me to write. How are you all? Are you busy as usual? Does Tim still work hard for his exam next month? I am miss you a lot and also all my friends from my English class. Yesterday I've received a letter from my Greece friend, Christina, and she told about some of the other students. She say that Atsuko and Yuki will write me from Japan. I am lucky because I made so many good friend during I was in Chicago. It was really interesting for me to meet people from so many different countries. I think that we not only improved our English (I hope this!) but we also knew people from all over the world and this is important.

My family are fine. They had a good summer vacation by the lake. We are all very exciting because my brother will get married just before Christmas and we like very much his girlfriend. They have looked for an apartment near the city center but it is no easy to find one. If they won't find one soon, they will have to stay here with us.

Please can you check something for me? I can't find my red scarf. I think maybe I have forgotten it in the closet in my bedroom.

Please write soon. My family send best wishes to you all. I hope I can come back next year. Stay with you was a very wonderful experience for me. Thank you for all things and excuse my mistakes. I already forget so much words.

Love,

Ana

p.s. I hope you like the photo. It's nice, isn't it?

2 Compare the mistakes you have found with a partner. Correct the letter.

3 Write a thank you letter to someone you have stayed with.

Tapescripts

Unit 7

T 7.1 **The job interview, part 1**

G = George Butler   H = Heather Mann
G Who do you work for now, Heather?
H I work for Intertec Publishing. We publish international business magazines.
G I see. And how long have you worked there?
H I've worked there for five years. Yes, exactly five years.
G And how long have you been in charge of East Asia publications?
H For two years.
G And what did you do before you were at Intertec?
H I worked as an interpreter for the United Nations.

T 7.2 **The job interview, part 2**

G = George Butler   H = Heather Mann
G As you know, this job is based in Santiago, Chile. Have you ever lived abroad before?
H Oh, yes. Yes, I have.
G And when did you live abroad?
H Well, in fact, I was born in Colombia and I lived there until I was 11. Also, I lived in Geneva for one year when I was working for the UN.
G That's interesting. Have you traveled much?
H Oh, yes. I've traveled to most countries in South America and many countries in Europe. I've also been to Japan a few times.
G Interesting. Why did you go to Japan?
H It was for my job. I went there to interview some Japanese business leaders.

T 7.3 **Listen and check**

1. She was born in Colombia in 1973.
2. She went to school in Bogota from 1978 to 1984.
3. She studied business and journalism at Boston University.
4. She worked in Geneva for a year before she worked for Intertec.
5. She's been to Japan a few times.
6. She's worked for Intertec for the last five years.
7. She hasn't lived abroad since she was in Geneva
8. She hasn't gotten a job at Worldwatch Americas yet.

T 7.4 **It's in the news**

Here are today's news headlines. … Convicted murderer Dwayne Locke has escaped from the Greenville Correctional Facility in Texas. … Two Spanish novelists have been awarded the Nobel Prize in literature. … Hurricane Jeffrey has hit the Caribbean, causing widespread damage in Puerto Rico. … Two thousand hotel workers in Anaheim, California have been laid off due to a slowdown in tourism. … Desmond Lewis has been knocked out in the fifth round of his heavyweight championship fight in Las Vegas.

T 7.5 **News stories**

1. The murderer Dwayne Locke has been recaptured by city police.
2. A Sunny Vacations cruise ship has sunk off the coast of Florida, near Miami.
3. Maria Martin, the famous movie star, has left $3 million to her pet cat, Fluffy.
4. A priceless Van Gogh painting has been stolen from the Museum of Modern Art in New York City.
5. Typhoon Ling-ling has killed at least 20 people and left 13,000 homeless in Vietnam.
6. An 18-year-old college student has been elected mayor of a town in California.
7. Senator Bill Smith has been forced to resign because of a financial scandal.
8. The world-champion runner Ken Quicksilver has failed a drug test at the Olympic Games and is expected to be disqualified.

T 7.6 **The busy life of a retired man**

P = Patti   L = Lou Norris
P How long have you been retired now, Grandpa?
L Let me see. It's been four years. Yup, I've been retired nearly four years now. But, you know, I worked for Siemco for nearly 40 years. Can you believe that? Forty years.
P One job for 40 years? Awesome! Don't you miss it? Don't you get bored?
L Ah, well, I'm lucky, I'm still healthy, so I can do a lot. I go out a lot. I've taken up golf, you know. It's a wonderful sport for an old guy like me because it's not really a sport at all, at least not the way your Grandpa plays it! It's just a good excuse for a walk, and I need an excuse since Bobby died. I miss good old Bobby, he and I were great pals … but I don't want another dog at my age. I go to the golf club twice a week. I've made some good friends there, you know. Have you met my friends Ted and Marjorie? They're my age. They're a really nice couple.
P No … I don't think I've met them. Didn't you go on vacation with them?
L Yes, I did. We went to Florida together last year. Oh … we had a great time, a real good time. They've been so kind to me since your Grandma died … you know, I really miss your Grandma. Thirty-five years we were married, 35 years. She was a wonderful lady, your Grandma.
P Oh, I know that, Grandpa. We all miss her a lot.
L Anyway, I like to keep busy. I like to travel and visit family and old friends.
P Mom says you went to visit Uncle Eric in Ohio.
L Oh, yeah. Last month. You have a new baby cousin, you know.
P I know, I haven't seen her yet. What's she like?
L She's beautiful. You'll love her. They named her Jessica, after your Grandma, and she looks just like your Grandma. She really does.
P I'd love to see her … But we never go anywhere. Dad's always working.
L Hey, he has a tough job, your dad. It's not his fault.
P Yeah, right. So, have you been anywhere else, Grandpa?

L Oh, well, I did go on a cruise around the Caribbean. My, that was an experience. I enjoyed every minute! When you're older I'll tell you about the widow from California that I met! Her name was Miriam, just 50 years old, but we got along really well together. Yes, indeed.

P Grandpa!

L Oh, sorry, I was just …

P Grandpa, next time you go away, please think of me. Can't I come with you? I'd love to travel. You and I could travel around Europe together. I'd take care of you!

L Patti, you know your Mom and Dad wouldn't let me. Not until you've finished school.

P Well, I think *you* have a lot more fun than I do! All I have to look forward to is years and years of school, and then years and years of work!

L Oh, Patti. Don't wish your life away. Just enjoy it all. You're 16. Sixteen. Ah, yes … Now, I can remember when I was 16, I …

T 7.7   Leaving a phone message

1. **A** Hello. May I speak to Arthur Lee, please?
   B I'm sorry. He's in a meeting right now. Can I take a message?
   A Yes. This is Pam Haddon. Mr. Lee called me earlier and left a message. I'm just returning his call. Can you please tell him that I'm back in my office now?
2. **A** Hello. This is Ray Gervin. May I speak to Janet Wolf, please?
   B I'm sorry, Mr. Gervin. She's away from her desk at the moment. Would you like Ms. Wolf to call you when she gets back?
   A Yes. If you don't mind. Let me give you my number. It's 619-555-3153.
3. **A** Hello. May I speak to Douglas Ryan, please?
   B One moment, please. … I'm sorry, but he's on another line. Do you want to hold?
   A No. That's OK. I'll call back later.

Unit 8

T 8.1   Jim goes backpacking, part 1

M = Mom   J = Jim

M Oh, dear, I hope everything will be all right. You've never been out of the country before.

J Don't worry, Mom. I'll be OK. I can take care of myself. Anyway, I'll be with Frank. We won't do anything stupid.

M But what will you do if you run out of money?

J We'll get jobs, of course!

M Oh? What if you get lost?

J Mom! If we get lost, we'll ask someone for directions, but we won't get lost because we know where we're going!

M Well, OK. … But what if you … ?

T 8.2   Jim goes backpacking, part 2

M = Mom   J = Jim

M But how will we know if you're all right?

J When we get to a city, I'll send you an e-mail.

M But, Jim, it's such a long flight to Madrid!

J Look, as soon as we arrive in Spain, I'll call you.

M I'll be worried until I hear from you.

J I'll be OK. Really!

T 8.3   The interview

J = Joe   S = Sue

J Bye, Honey! Good luck with the interview!

S Thanks. I'll need it. I hope the trains are running on time. If I'm late for the interview, I'll be furious with myself!

J Just stay calm! Call me when you can.

S I will. I'll call you on my cell phone as soon as I get out of the interview.

J When will you know if you have the job?

S They'll tell me in the next few days. If they offer me the job, I'm going to accept it. You know that, don't you?

J Sure. But we'll worry about that later.

S OK. Are you going to work now?

J Well, I'm going to take the kids to school before I go to work.

S Don't forget to pick them up before you come home.

J Don't worry, I won't forget. You'd better get going. If you don't hurry, you'll miss the train.

S OK. I'll see you this evening. Bye!

T 8.4   Winning the lottery

1. What would I do if I won $5 million? Well, I'd make sure my family had enough money, and my friends, and I'd give a load of money to charity. And then I'd buy my own island in the Caribbean.
2. If I won $5 million, I'd spend it all on myself. Every last cent!
3. What would I do? I'd buy a nice house in the country. I'd make it the best place I could. And I'd have lots of land, so I could have peace and quiet.
4. I'd be a space tourist and fly to Mars on the space shuttle.
5. Oh, that's easy! I'd quit my job and travel. Anywhere. Everywhere. But it wouldn't change me. I'd still live in the same neighborhood because I like it so much.

T 8.5   Listen and check

1. If Tony calls, tell him I'm at Alex's. He can reach me there.
2. If you've finished your work, you can take a break. Just be back in 15 minutes.
3. If I'm not back by 8 P.M., don't wait for me. Go without me and I'll meet you at the party.
4. If you have the flu, you should go to bed. Keep warm and drink plenty of fluids.
5. If you're ever in Vancouver, please let me know. I'd love to show you around.
6. If you go to Brazil, you have to have a visa. You can get one at the embassy.
7. I'd buy a computer if I could afford it. It would be really useful for work.
8. If I had more time, I might take an evening class. I'd love to learn more about photography.

T 8.6   "Who wants to be a millionaire?"

Who wants to be a millionaire?
I don't.
Have flashy flunkies everywhere.
I don't.
Who wants the bother of a country estate?
A country estate is something I'd hate.

Who wants to wallow in champagne?
I don't.
Who wants a supersónic plane?
I don't.
Who wants a private landing field too?
I don't.
And I don't cuz all I want is you.

Who wants to be a millionaire?
I don't.
Who wants uranium to spare?
I don't.
Who wants to journey on a gigantic yacht?
Do I want a yacht? Oh, how I do not!

Who wants a fancy foreign car?
I don't.
Who wants to tire of caviar?
I don't.
Who wants a marble swimming pool, too?
I don't.
And I don't cuz all I want is you.

T 8.7   Base and strong adjectives

1. **A** What did you do last night?
   B We went to the movies.
   A What did you see?
   B *Murder in the Park.*
   A Was it good?
   B It was absolutely superb!
2. **A** Is it true that Liz won the lottery?
   B Yes! She won $2 million!
   A I'll bet she was really happy.
   B Happy? She was absolutely thrilled!
3. **A** When I got home, I told my parents that I'd failed the exam.
   B Oh, no! What did they say?
   A My Mom was OK, but my Dad was really furious.
4. **A** We went out for dinner at that new restaurant last night.
   B Oh! Was it any good?
   A No! It was awful!
5. **A** We had a wonderful skiing trip last weekend.
   B Oh, yeah? Was the weather good?
   A It was absolutely fantastic!
6. **A** How long was your flight?
   B Fourteen hours.
   A Fourteen hours! You must be really tired.
   B Yeah. I'm absolutely exhausted!

T 8.8   Charity appeals

Amnesty International

Amnesty International is a Nobel Prize–winning organization that works to support human rights around the world. It is independent of any government or political party and has over a million members in 162 countries around the world. Amnesty International works to free all prisoners of conscience anywhere in the world. These are people who are in prison because of their beliefs, color, ethnic origin, language, or religion. Amnesty International tries to help these prisoners in two ways. First, by publicizing their cases and, second, by putting pressure on governments to practice human rights.

The World Wildlife Fund

The World Wildlife Fund is the largest privately supported international conservation organization in the world. It is dedicated to protecting wild animals around the world and the places where these animals live. The World Wildlife Fund directs its conservation efforts toward three global goals. First, it works to save endangered species like the black rhino or the giant panda. Second, it works to establish and manage national parks and wildlife reserves around the world. Third, it works to address global threats to our environment, such as pollution and climate change.

Save the Children

Millions of children around the world experience lives filled with poverty, disease, war, violence, and discrimination. Save the Children believes that children, wherever they live, have the right to a happy, healthy, and secure start in life, and is committed to turning this ideal into a reality for all children. Save the Children helps children by supporting programs that involve community members in improving their day-to-day lives, such as maternal and child healthcare services, education for all children, and income-earning opportunities for women. Save the Children also uses its global experience and research to help children and families during natural disasters and times of war, as well as to advocate for government policy changes that will benefit all children, including future generations.

T 8.9 Making suggestions

M = Maria   A = Anna

M I'm bored!
A Well, it's a beautiful day. Why don't we go for a walk?
M No, I don't feel like it. I'm too tired.
A You need to get out. Let's go shopping!
M Oh, no! I'd rather do anything but that.
A OK … How about watching TV?
M That's a good idea.
A Do you want to watch the news?
M Mmm, I'd rather watch *The Simpsons*.

P = Paul   B = Bill

P I'm broke, and I don't get paid for two weeks. What am I going to do?
B If I were you, I'd get a better job.
P Oh, why didn't I think of that? Thanks, Bill. That's a big help.
B Well, you'd better get a loan from the bank.
P No, I can't. I owe them too much already.
B Why don't you ask your parents? They'd help you out.
P No, I'd rather not. I'd rather work out my problems myself.
B You ought to ask your boss for a raise!
P Good idea, but I've already tried that and it didn't work.
B Oh. Well, I suppose I could lend you some money.
P Really? That would be great! Thanks, Bill. You're a real pal.
B Yeah, well, just one thing: I don't think you should spend so much. That way, you won't be broke all the time.
P Yeah, yeah. I know. You're right.

Unit 9

T 9.1 Listen and check

1. A I haven't eaten anything since breakfast.
   B You must be hungry.
2. A Bob works three jobs.
   B He can't have much free time.
3. A The phone's ringing.
   B It might be Jane.
4. A Paula's umbrella is soaking wet!
   B It must be raining.
5. A Listen to all those fire engines!
   B There must be a fire somewhere.
6. A I don't know where Sam is.
   B He could be in his bedroom.
7. A Marta isn't in the kitchen.
   B She can't be cooking dinner.
8. A Whose coat is this?
   B It might be John's.

T 9.2 What are they talking about?

Conversation 1
A It's Father's Day next Sunday.
B I know. Should we buy Dad a present or just send him a card?

Conversation 2
A One coffee and a sparkling mineral water, please.
B Would you like lemon with the mineral water?
A Yes. And can we order dinner now?
B Yes, of course.

Conversation 3
I don't work regular hours and I like that. I'd hate one of those nine-to-five office jobs. Also I meet a lot of really interesting people. Of course, every now and then there's a difficult customer, but most times people are really nice. I took that really famous movie star to the airport last week, now what was her name? … Anyway, she was real nice. Gave me a big tip!

Conversation 4
A So, how did it go?
B I'm not sure. I think it went OK.
A Were you nervous?
B Yeah, very, but I tried not to show it.
A Could you answer all their questions?
B Most of them.
A What happens now?
B Well, they said they'd call me in a couple of days and let me know if I got it.

Conversation 5
A We've never had one before.
B Really? We've always had them in our family. We're all crazy about them.
A Well, we are now. The kids love her. And she is so good with them, very good-natured. But it wasn't fair to have one when we lived in an apartment.
B It's OK if they're small and you live near a park, but I know what you mean. What's her name?
A Trudi.

T 9.3 See p. 68

T 9.4 A vacation with friends

A = Andy   C= Carl

A Hi! Carl? It's Andy. How are you? Doing better?
C Uh … not really. I have to sit down most of the time. It's too tiring—walking with these crutches.
A Really? Still on crutches, eh? So you're not back at work yet?
C No. And I'm really bored. I don't go back to see the doctor for another week.
A Another week! Is that when the cast comes off?
C I hope so. I can't wait to have two legs again! Anyway, how are you? Do you miss the snow and the mountains?
A I'm fine. We're both fine. Julie sends her love, by the way.
C Thanks. I miss you all. By the way, have you gotten any of your photos back yet?
A Yes, yes, we have. Julie picked them up today. They're good. I didn't realize we'd taken so many of us all.
C What about that one with the fantastic sunset behind the hotel?
A Yes, the sunset? It's beautiful. All of us together on Bob and Marcia's balcony, with the mountains and the snow in the background. It brings back memories.
C Yeah. The memory of me skiing into a tree!
A Yes, I know. I'm sorry. But at least it happened at the end; it could have been the first day. You only missed the last two days.
C OK, OK. Oh, Andy, have you written to the hotel yet to complain about your room? That view you had over the parking lot was awful!
A Yeah, and it was noisy, too! We didn't have any views of the mountains from our room. Yeah, we've written. We e-mailed the manager yesterday, but I don't know if we'll get any money back.
C And Marcia's suitcase, did she find it?
A Yeah. The airline found it and put it on the next flight. Marcia was very relieved.
C I'll bet she was! All in all I suppose it was a pretty good vacation, wasn't it?
A Absolutely. It was a *great* vacation. Some ups and downs, but we all had fun. Should we go again next year?
C I'd like to. All six of us again. Lisa wants to go again, too. It was her first time skiing and she loved it, but she says she'll only come if I don't break a leg!
A Great! It's a date. Next time go around the trees! I'll call you again soon, Carl. Take care!
C You too, Andy. Bye now.
A Bye.

T 9.5 Listen and check

1. A I can't find my ticket.
   B You must have dropped it.
2. A Mark didn't come to school last week.
   B He must have been sick.
3. A Why is Isabel late for class?
   B She might have overslept.
4. A I can't find my homework.
   B You must have forgotten it.
5. A The teacher's checking Maria's work.
   B She can't have finished already!
6. A How did Bob get such a good grade on that test?
   B He must have cheated!

T 9.6 Brothers and sisters

Luisa

I = Interviewer   L = Luisa

I Luisa, tell me about your family.

L I'm the youngest of seven children. My oldest sister is still alive, age 93, and there are 16 years between us. There were four girls, two boys, and then me.

I Seven children! Wow! How did you all get along?

L Very well. Very well. Being the youngest, my two young brothers and I called our older sisters "the others," because they were either married or working by the time we were born. But the seven of us all got along very well. But it's different now, of course.

I Really? How so?

L Well, when we were small, my older sisters often took care of us. Now my brothers and I are busy taking care of them.

I Tell me about your big sister, Julia. How has your relationship with her changed over the years?

L Julia was the sister who used to … on her vacations … used to take me for walks and so forth. But then she became a nun and went to Brazil for 23 years. We wrote to one another and I was still her little sister. When she came back, it was shortly after my husband died, we became very close and our whole relationship changed and we became great friends.

I What do you see as the main advantage and disadvantage of coming from such a large family?

L Hmm. I think the main advantage was that we learned how to enjoy life without having a lot of money. I think our other relatives, my rich cousins in the city, envied us. We had old bikes, old clothes, but we also had lots of freedom. In the city, they had to wear nice suits and behave correctly.

I Hmm. Disadvantages?

L I think it was very difficult sometimes to have hand-me-down clothes, especially for a little girl like me. And I was sad that we didn't go away on vacation like some other children. But the advantages outweighed the disadvantages enormously, there's no doubt about that.

I Six out of the seven of you are still alive. How closely have you kept in touch over the years?

L Very closely. Of course, we still call each other all the time and see each other whenever we can. And we have a big family reunion every year. My granddaughter just had twins. That means we'll have four generations there this year. How marvelous!

Rose

I = Interviewer   R = Rose

I So, Rose, do you have any brothers or sisters?

R No, I don't. I'm an only child.

I So what was it like growing up as an only child? Were you happy?

R When I was little, I liked it. I had lots of cousins and most of them lived in the same town, so we all played together all the time. And I had a best friend who lived next door to me. She was the same age as me and so she was kind of like a sister, I suppose. But she moved away and that was sad. It was hard when I was a teenager.

I How so?

R Well, you know how it is being a teenager. You're kind of unsure of how to deal with things and how to deal with people, especially parents. It would have been nice to have a brother or sister to talk to.

I Some people who come from large families might envy you, because you had all of your parents' attention.

R Yes, but I think that has its negatives as well as its positives. I think you don't want all your parents' attention, especially as a teenager. It was hard to find myself and my place in the world, I guess.

I What about now that you're an adult?

R Again, I think it's difficult really. Mmm … my father died about ten years ago, so of course I'm the one who's left totally responsible for my mother. I'm the one who has to take care of her if she has a problem and help her if she needs help in any way. There's nobody else to help at all.

I You're married now with two children of your own. Was that a conscious decision to have more than one child?

R Yes, very definitely. And they seem very happy and they get along very well with one another. Usually.

T 9.7 So do I! Neither do I!

A–J = Sue's friends   S = Sue

1. **A** I want to travel the world.
   S So do I.
2. **B** I don't want to have lots of children.
   S Neither do I.
3. **C** I can speak four languages.
   S I can't.
4. **D** I can't drive.
   S Neither can I.
5. **E** I'm not going to get married until I'm 35.
   S Neither am I.
6. **F** I went to London last year.
   S So did I.
7. **G** I've never been to Australia.
   S I have.
8. **H** I don't like politicians.
   S Neither do I.
9. **I** I'm bored with Hollywood actors.
   S So am I.
10. **J** I love going to parties.
    S So do I.

Unit 10

T 10.1 Asking questions

1. How long has he been learning to drive?
2. How many driving lessons has he had?
3. How much money has he spent on driving lessons?
4. How many different instructors has he had?
5. How many times has he crashed his car?
6. When did he start learning to drive?
7. How many times has he taken his driving test?
8. How has he been celebrating?

T 10.2 See p. 75

T 10.3 Listen and check

1. **A** You're covered in paint! What have you been doing?
   B I've been redecorating the bathroom.
   A Have you finished yet?
   B Well, I've painted the door, but I haven't put up the wallpaper yet.
2. **A** Your hands are really dirty. What have you been doing?
   B They're filthy. I've been working in the garden.
   A Have you finished yet?
   B Well, I've cut the grass, but I haven't watered the flowers yet.
3. **A** Your eyes are red! What have you been doing?
   B I'm exhausted. I've been studying for my final exams.
   A Have you finished yet?
   B Well, I've finished chemistry and history, but I haven't started English yet.

T 10.4 Questions and answers

1. **A** When was she born?
   B In 1960.
2. **A** When was her collection of poems published?
   B In April 1968, when she was eight years old.
3. **A** When did she get married for the first time?
   B In the spring of 1981, when she was 21.
4. **A** What did she major in at Columbia?
   B English literature.
5. **A** Which countries has she been to?
   B She's been to Ireland, France, Spain, China, Japan, and Vietnam.
6. **A** How long did her first marriage last?
   B Eight years.
7. **A** When did she get married for the second time?
   B On August 3, 1998.
8. **A** How long has she been living in southern California?
   B Since 1998.

1. I How long are you here in Britain for?
   E Just two weeks.
2. I How long have you been in Britain?
   E Eight days.
3. I When do you go back to California?
   E On Saturday.
5. I Where were you the day before yesterday?
   E In Birmingham.
6. I Where were you this time last week?
   E In London.
7. I Where will you be the day after tomorrow?
   E I'll be in Edinburgh.

T 10.6 The doll collector

I = Interviewer   A = Andrea Levitt

I First of all, just a little bit about you. Are you originally from New York City?
A I'm from Wilmington, Delaware, but I've been living in New York a long time. I came to New York to work in the fashion industry. I still work in the world of fashion. I love it.
I So, how long have you been collecting dolls?
A Hmm … it must be about 25 years. Yeah, 25 years.
I So what led you to having such a love of dolls? Have you always loved them?
A Well, no. I didn't play with dolls much when I was a kid, but these aren't kids' dolls that I collect.
I No?
A No, they're really works of art. When you say the word "doll" people think of a toy for little girls, but these are not. When I opened my business, Dolls-at-Home, one year ago, that was the message I wanted to get across to all art lovers—that dolls are another art form.
I I can see that these are not dolls for little girls. Some of them are really quite amazing. How many dolls do you have in your collection?
A Oooh, I would say … hmm, I think maybe 300.
I Wow! And where are they all?
A Well, I had to buy a new apartment …
I You bought an apartment for the dolls?!
A Yeah, I really did. My son, he's 31 now, he went off to college and I filled his room with dolls in 2 minutes so I realized that I needed a different apartment. I wanted to show off my dolls.
I So, you have what, maybe four or five rooms, all with dolls …
A Actually, there are dolls in *every* room, even the bathroom and the kitchen.
I I was going to ask, is there one room where you don't allow dolls?
A No! Oh, no, they're part of my life. I mean sometimes when people visit there's nowhere to sit. It's a problem.
I Hmm. So, what about keeping them clean? Dusting them?
A That's a problem too. New York is dirty. I suppose they should be under glass, but I don't want them under glass, I want to enjoy them. I dust them occasionally.
I Well, they look immaculate.
A Thanks.
I That's a very unusual doll. Is it valuable?
A No, not really. But that doll over there … It has an elephant mask? That's my favorite.
I Oh, really?

A You see the mask goes up and it's a little boy's face …
I Oh.
A And it goes down and it's an elephant's face. It's made by one of the best doll makers in the US, Akira Blount.
I And how do you find your dolls?
A I travel all over. I go to doll shows, and now that I have a web site and I've started my own business, doll artists find me. As I said, it's been going on for a year now, and I have a mailing list of 900 people.
I Wow! What does your son think of all this?
A You know, he thinks I'm sort of … crazy. He loves this apartment, but he just can't understand …
I Why you fill it with dolls!
A Yeah, but two weeks ago he came to one of my doll shows, it was his first time, and I think he was impressed. Yeah, I think so.
I Do you think you'll ever stop collecting them?
A No, there's always room for another doll. If you're a real collector you always find room.
I Hmm, I'm sure you're right. That's great Andrea. Thank you very much.

T 10.7 The *Star Wars* collector

I = Interviewer   J = Jeff Parker

I First of all, just a little bit about you, Jeff. Are you originally from New York City?
J No, I'm originally from the Philadelphia area. But I moved to New York about five years ago when I got a job working for a bank on Wall Street.
I And do you mind talking about your *Star Wars* collection?
J No, not at all.
I So, how did you get interested in *Star Wars*?
J Well, *Star Wars* was one of the first movies I ever saw. I think I was four years old. My Dad took me to see it and I just loved it. Loved the story, loved the idea of being in space. I think I saw it ten times.
I Wow! You sure did love *Star Wars*!
J Yeah, I guess so. And then all the toys came out, so I started collecting the action figures.
I Action figures?
J They're these little metallic figures. Models of the characters in the movie.
I I see. And which character did you like best?
J Oh, I was a Han Solo fan. I think he was my favorite. You know, I still have that Han Solo action figure. It's worth a lot of money now, but I like it because it was the first *Star Wars* thing I ever owned.
I So, did you just collect the figures?
J Oh, no. I collected the figures first—Darth Vader, Luke, Obi-Wan Kenobi, R2-D2, and of course, Princess Leia.
I Uh-huh.
J Then I just started collecting everything *Star Wars*—spaceships, space stations, posters, videos …
I Well, you seem to have a lot of pieces in your collection. About how many pieces do you have all together?
J I'm not sure because most of my collection is at my parents' house in Philadelphia.
I Ah.
J I don't have room for all of it here in New York … but I'd say I probably have about 700 pieces in all.

I Seven hundred pieces!? How did you get so many?
J Well, you know, I'd ask my Mom for the newest toys—every holiday, every birthday—and the collection just grew and grew. I think they really liked *Star Wars*, too. When I was a kid my Mom gave me *Star Wars* birthday parties, and bought me *Star Wars* cereal for breakfast … I even had *Star Wars* pajamas and *Star Wars* underwear.
I Aha. A real *Star Wars* family then?
J You could say that. We even called our family dog Princess Leia.
I And did you play with other kids who collected *Star Wars* stuff?
J No, not really. I liked to play with all the things by myself. I loved making up all these *Star Wars* stories about the characters …
I And now? Are you in touch with other *Star Wars* collectors?
J No. I don't have the time really.
I So, what are you going to do with your collection?
J I don't know. I'm not sure. Sometimes I think I might sell it. Other times I think I might just keep it and give it to my kids someday.
I That would be something, wouldn't it? Thanks, Jeff.

T 10.8 Expressing quantity

1. A How much coffee do you drink?
   B At least six cups a day.
   A That's too much. You shouldn't drink as much as that.
2. A Do we have any sugar?
   B Yes, but not enough. We need some more.
3. A How much do you earn?
   B Not enough to pay all my bills!
4. A How many people are there in your class?
   B Forty.
   A I think that's too many.
5. A How many aspirins do you usually take when you have a headache?
   B About four or five.
   A That's too many. You shouldn't take as many as that!
6. A How old are you?
   B Seventeen. I'm old enough to get married, but not old enough to vote!
7. A When did you last go to the movies?
   B Pretty recently. Just a few days ago.
8. A Do you take milk in your coffee?
   B Just a little.

Unit 11

T 11.1   **The first day of vacation**

F = Flavia   C = Hotel concierge

F   Hi. I've just checked in and I wonder if you could help me.
C   I'll be happy to try.
F   Well, first, I'm not sure if we're near the CN Tower.
C   The CN Tower? It's very close. It's only about a ten-minute walk.
F   Oh, good. Can you tell me if there are any good restaurants nearby?
C   Lots. One good one is the Cafe Giovanni. It's casual, but they have very good food and live music in the evenings.
F   Sounds wonderful. Oh, and I need to cash some traveler's checks, but I don't know when the banks are open.
C   Most banks are open from 8:30 A.M. till 5:30 P.M. on weekdays, but some have extended hours.
F   Thank you very much. Oh … I'm sorry, but I can't remember which restaurant you suggested.
C   The Cafe Giovanni.
F   Cafe Giovanni. Got it. Thanks for your help.
C   My pleasure.

T 11.2   see p. 84

T 11.3   **Listen and check**

K=Karen   A = Karen's Assistant

K   Now, what's happening today? I have a meeting this afternoon, don't I?
A   Yes, that's right. With Henry and Tom.
K   And the meeting's here, isn't it?
A   No, it isn't. It's in Tom's office at 3:00 P.M.
K   Oh! I'm not having lunch with anyone, am I?
A   No, you're free for lunch.
K   Phew! And I signed all my letters, didn't I?
A   No, you didn't, actually. They're on your desk, waiting for you.
K   OK. I'll do them now. Thanks a lot.

T 11.4   **Question tags and intonation**

1. It isn't very warm today, is it?
2. You can cook, can't you?
3. You have a CD player, don't you?
4. Mary's very smart, isn't she?
5. There are a lot of people here, aren't there?
6. The movie wasn't very good, was it?
7. I'm next in line, aren't I?
8. You aren't going out dressed like that, are you?

T 11.5   **Listen and check**

1. **A**   It isn't very warm today, is it?
    B   No, it's freezing.
2. **A**   You can cook, can't you?
    B   Me? No! I can't even boil an egg.
3. **A**   You have a CD player, don't you?
    B   Believe it or not, I don't. I have a cassette player, though.
4. **A**   Mary's very smart, isn't she?
    B   Yes. She's extremely bright.
5. **A**   There are a lot of people here, aren't there?
    B   I know! It's absolutely packed! I can't move!

6. **A**   The movie wasn't very good, was it?
    B   It was terrible! The worst I've seen in ages.
7. **A**   I'm next in line, aren't I?
    B   Yes, you are. You'll be called next.
8. **A**   You aren't going out dressed like that, are you?
    B   Why? What's wrong with my clothes? I thought I looked really cool.

T 11.6   **Add the question tags**

A   It's so romantic, isn't it?
B   What is?
A   Well, they're really in love, aren't they?
B   Who?
A   Paul and Mary.
B   Paul and Mary aren't in love, are they?
A   Oh, yes, they are. They're crazy about each other.

T 11.7   **Listen and check**

1. **A**   You broke that vase, didn't you?
    B   Yes, I did. I dropped it. I'm sorry.
    A   You'll replace it, won't you?
    B   Yes, of course I will. How much did it cost?
    A $300.
    B $300?! It *wasn't* that much, was it?
    A   Yes, it *was*.
2. **A**   Did you pay the electric bill?
    B   No, *you* paid it, didn't you?
    A   No, I didn't pay it. I thought you paid it.
    B   Me? You *always* pay it, don't you?
    A   No, I don't. I always pay the phone bill.
    B   Oh, that's right.
3. **A**   We love each other, don't we?
    B   Um, I think so.
    A   We don't ever want to be apart, do we?
    B   Well …
    A   And we'll get married and have lots of children, won't we?
    B   What? You didn't buy me a ring, did you?
    A   Yes, I did. Diamonds are forever.
    B   Oh, no!
4. **A**   Helen didn't win the lottery, did she?
    B   Yes, she did. She won $4 million!
    A   She isn't going to give it all to charity, is she?
    B   As a matter of fact, she is.
    A   Wow. Not many people would do that, would they?
    B   Well, *I* certainly wouldn't.
5. **A**   I think we're lost. Let's look at the map.
    B   Uh-oh.
    A   What do you mean, "Uh-oh"? You didn't forget the map, did you?
    B   Sorry.
    A   How are we going to get back to the campground without a map?
    B   Well, we could ask a police officer, couldn't we?
    A   There aren't many police officers on this mountain!

T 11.8   **The forgetful generation, part 1**

Hi, and welcome to "What's Your Problem?" How's your day been so far? Have you done all the things you planned? Kept all your appointments? Oh—and did you remember to send your mother a birthday card? If so, good for you! If not—well, you're not alone. Many of us in the busy twenty-first century are

finding it more and more difficult to remember everything. Once upon a time we just blamed getting older for our absent-mindedness, but now experts are blaming our modern lifestyle. They say that we have become "the forgetful generation" and that day after day we overload our memories.

T 11.9   **The forgetful generation, part 2**

LeeAnn
Last year I graduated from college and I got a job in the same town. One day, for some reason, instead of going to work, which starts at nine o'clock, I took the bus and went to the university for an eleven o'clock lecture. I was sitting there, in the lecture room, and I thought to myself, "Why don't I know anybody?" Then suddenly I remembered that I'd graduated already and that I was two hours late for work!

Jerry
I live and work in Chicago. Last Christmas I packed my suitcase as I do every year and went to the airport to catch a flight to my parents' home for the holidays. While I was standing in line waiting to check in, one of the people from the airline came by to check my ticket. He looked at it and said, "Thank you, sir. Your flight to Kansas City leaves in about an hour." And suddenly I thought, "Kansas City? But I don't want to go to Kansas City. My parents live in Arizona!" You see, when I was a child I lived with my parents in Kansas City, but they moved to Arizona seven years ago. I couldn't believe it. I'd bought an airline ticket to the wrong city! How could I have been so stupid?

Keiko
A few months ago I got up to go to work. I got dressed and put on my nice blue suit because I had an important meeting. I'd been working at home the night before and preparing for a very important meeting the next day, and I remembered to put all the right papers into my briefcase. I got in my car and drove to work. When I arrived I looked down—I was shocked. I was still wearing my fluffy, pink bedroom slippers!

T 11.10   **The forgetful generation, part 3**

P = Presenter   A = Alan Buchan

P   Stories of forgetfulness like these are familiar to many of us, and experts say that such cases as LeeAnn's, Jerry's, and Keiko's show that loss of memory is not just related to age, but can be caused by our way of life. Alan Buchan is a professor of psychology and he explains why.
A   One of the problems, these days, is that many companies have far fewer employees. This means that *one* person often does several jobs. Jobs that before were done by many people are now done by a few. If you have five things to do at once, you become stressed and forgetful. I think many people in work situations, at a meeting or something, have the experience where they start a sentence and half way through it, they can't remember what they're talking about, and they can't finish the sentence.
P   That's happened to me.

A It's a terrible feeling—you think you're going insane. I remember one lady who came to me so distressed because at three important meetings in one week, she found herself saying, mid-sentence, "I'm sorry, I can't remember what I'm talking about." This was a lady in a new job, which involved a lot of traveling. She also had a home and family to take care of *and* she'd recently moved. She had so *many* things to think about that her brain couldn't cope. It shut down.

P I can see the problem, but what's the solution? How did you help that lady?

A Well, part of the solution is recognizing the problem. Once we'd talked to this lady about her stressful lifestyle, she realized that she wasn't going crazy and she felt more relaxed and was able to help herself. But do you know one of the best ways to remember things, even in these days of personal computers and handheld computers?

P What's that?

A It's a notebook, or just a piece of paper! At the beginning of every day write yourself a list of things you have to do—and it gives you a really good feeling when you cross things off the list as you do them!

P Well, there you have it! Thank you very much Professor … uh … uh … ? Oh—Professor Alan Buchan!

T 11.11 Informal English

1. A What do you say we take a break for lunch?
   B Great idea. We can grab a sandwich at the deli.
2. A What are you up to?
   B Nothing much. Just sitting around, watching TV all weekend.
   A You're such a couch potato!
   B Hey, give me a break. I work hard all week. I like to chill out in front of the TV.
3. A Quick! Give me your homework so I can copy it.
   B No way! Do your own homework!
4. A Did you fix the TV?
   B Kind of. The picture's OK, but the sound isn't quite right.
   A What's on tonight?
   B Beats me. Did you look in the paper?
5. A What do you call that stuff that you use to clean between your teeth?
   B What do you mean?
   A You know! It's like string. White.
   B Oh! You mean dental floss.
   A Yeah. That's it!

Unit 12

T 12.1

E = Elliott   M = Martha
1. E How do you know Joel and Tara?
   M I studied at UCLA with Tara.
2. E Are you married?
   M Yes, I am. That's my husband over there.
3. E Where did you meet your husband?
   M Actually, I met him at a wedding.
4. E Have you traveled far to get here?
   M No, we haven't. We just got here yesterday. We flew in from Orlando.
5. E Do you live in Orlando?
   M Yes, we do.
6. E So, where are you staying in Atlanta?
   M We're staying at the Four Seasons Hotel.
7. E So am I. Can we meet there later for coffee?
   M Sure. I'll introduce you to my husband.

T 12.2 Listen and check

M = Martha   R = Ron
M I just met this really nice guy named Elliot.
R Oh, yeah?
M He was very friendly. Do you know what he said? First, he asked me how I knew Joel and Tara. I told him that I had studied with Tara at UCLA. Then he asked if I was married. Of course I said that I was!
R He asked you that?
M … and next he asked where we'd met. I told him that we'd actually met at a wedding.
R You told him that?
M Sure. Then he wanted to know how long we had been in Atlanta …
R Really?
M I said we had just gotten here yesterday, that we had flown in from Orlando.
R Uh-huh.
M He asked if we lived in Orlando, so I told him that we did.
R What else did this guy want to know?
M Well, he asked where we were staying in Atlanta and it turns out that he's staying at the Four Seasons, too.
R I see.
M Then he asked if I could meet him later for coffee …
R Mhmm.
M And I said we could and that I would introduce him to you.
R I'm not sure I want to meet this guy.

T 12.3 What did Elliott say?

R = Ron   M = Martha
1. R Elliot lives in Detroit.
   M But he told me he lived in New York.
2. R He doesn't like his new job.
   M But he said that he loved it!
3. R He's moving to Iowa.
   M But he told me he was moving to Florida!
4. R He stayed home on his last vacation.
   M But he told me he went to Paris!
5. R He'll be 40 next week.
   M But he told me he'd be 30!
6. R He's been married three times.
   M But he told me he'd never been married!
   R You see! I told you he was a liar!

T 12.4 Listen and check

1. The mail carrier told me to sign on the dotted line.
2. She asked him to translate a sentence for her.
3. She reminded him to send a birthday card.
4. He begged her to marry him.
5. He invited his boss to his wedding.
6. He refused to go to bed.
7. He advised him to talk to his lawyer.
8. The teacher ordered Joanna to take the chewing gum out of her mouth.

T 12.5 Kathleen Brady

OK. We argue sometimes but not *that* often. Usually we just sit quietly and watch TV in the evenings. But sometimes … sometimes we argue about money. We don't have much, so I get very upset when Kenny spends the little we have on drinking or gambling. He's promised to stop drinking, but he hasn't stopped. It's worse since he lost his job. OK, we were shouting, but we didn't throw a chair at Mr. West. It … it just fell out of the window. And I'm really sorry that we woke the baby. We won't do it again. We love children. We'll baby-sit for Mr. and Mrs. West anytime, if they want to go out.

T 12.6 Ann West

Every night it's the same thing. They argue all the time. And we can hear every word they say. During the day it's not so bad because they're both out. But in the evenings it's terrible. Usually they start arguing about which TV show to watch. Then he slams the door and goes down the street to a bar. Last night he came back really drunk. He was shouting outside his front door, "Open the door you … um … so-and-so." I won't tell you the language he used! But she wouldn't open it; she opened a window instead and threw a plant at him. Tonight she threw a chair at my poor husband. They're so selfish. They don't care about our baby one bit.

T 12.7 Great Aunt Dodi's birth

This story is told over and over again in our family. It's the story of how my Great Aunt Dodi was born twice. She was born on Prince Edward Island on January 16, 1910. She was the fourth of six children. It was January and really cold, freezing. The midwife only just managed to get there in time, through all the snow. When my great aunt was born she was blue, really blue, and she wasn't breathing at all and the midwife said, "Well, I'm terribly sorry, there's nothing we can do … I'm afraid the child isn't breathing."

But my great-grandmother stepped forward and said, "Nonsense! Give me that child!" And she grabbed the baby from the midwife and ran downstairs into the warm living room and then … incredibly … she opened the door of the wood stove and put the baby into the oven. And what do you know, a few minutes later a great loud cry came from the oven and my great aunt had been born, or rather, born again.

So that's how my Great Aunt Dodi was born twice. She's still alive and she never tires of telling the story of her birth to her five children, eleven grandchildren, and two great-grandchildren.

T 12.8 See p. 95

See p. 95

T 12.9 "My Way"

And now, the end is near
And so I face the final curtain
My friend, I'll say it clear
I'll state my case, of which I'm certain
I've lived a life that's full
I've traveled each and every highway
And more, much more than this,
I did it my way …

Regrets, I've had a few
But then again, too few to mention
I did what I had to do
and saw it through without exemption,
I planned each charted course,
each careful step along the byway
And more, much more than this,
I did it my way …

Yes, there were times,
I'm sure you knew,
When I bit off
more than I could chew
But through it all,
when there was doubt
I ate it up and spit it out
I faced it all and I stood tall
and did it my way …

I've loved, I've laughed and cried
I've had my fill, my share of losing
And now, as tears subside,
I find it all so amusing
To think I did all that
And may I say, not in a shy way,
"Oh, no, oh, no, not me, I did it my way.
For what is a man, what has he got?
If not himself, then he has naught.
To say the things he truly feels
and not the words of one who kneels,
The record shows I took the blows
and did it my way …
Yes, it was my way …

T 12.10 Saying sorry

1. **A** Excuse me, what's that creature called?
    B It's a Tyrannosaurus.
    A Pardon me?
    B A Tyrannosaurus. Tyrannosaurus Rex.
    A Thank you very much.
2. **A** Ouch! That's my foot!
    B Sorry. I wasn't looking where I was going.
3. **A** Excuse me, can you tell me where the post office is?
    B I'm sorry, I'm a stranger here myself.
4. **A** I failed my driving test for the sixth time!
    B I'm so sorry.
5. **A** Excuse me! We need to get past. My little boy isn't feeling well.
6. **A** Do you want your hearing aid, Grandma?
    B Pardon me?
    A I said: Do you want your hearing aid?
    B What?
    A DO YOU WANT YOUR HEARING AID?!
    B I'm sorry, I can't hear you. I need my hearing aid.

This page has been left blank.

Pages 136–144 (the Grammar Reference pages for Units 1–6)
appear in Student Book 3A.

Grammar Reference

Unit 7

Introduction to the Present Perfect

The same form (*have* + past participle) exists in many European languages, but the uses in English are different. In English, the Present Perfect is essentially a present tense, but it also expresses the effect of past actions and activities on the present.

Present Perfect means "before now." The Present Perfect does not express when an action happened. If we say the exact time, we have to use the Past Simple.

In my life, I **have traveled** to all seven continents.
I **traveled** around Africa **in 1998**.

7.1 The Present Perfect

Form

Affirmative and negative

I We You They	've haven't	lived in Rome.
He She	's hasn't	

Question

How long have	I we you	known Peter?
How long has	she he	

Short answer

Have you always lived in Chicago?	Yes, I have. No, I haven't.

Use

The Present Perfect expresses:
1. an action that began in the past and still continues (unfinished past).
   We**'ve lived** in the same house for 25 years.
   Peter**'s worked** as a teacher since 2000.
   How long **have** you **known** each other?
   They**'ve been** married for 20 years.

   ##### Note
   Many languages express this idea with a present tense, but in English this is wrong.
   Peter **has been** a teacher for ten years. NOT ~~Peter is a teacher for ten years.~~

These time expressions are common with this use.

for	two years a month a few minutes half an hour ages	since	1970 the end of the class August 8:00 Christmas

We use *for* with a period of time and *since* with a point in time.

2. an experience that happened at some time in one's life. The action is in the past and finished, but the effects of the action are still felt. When the action happened is not important.
   I**'ve been** to the United States. (I still remember.)
   She**'s written** poetry and children's stories. (in her writing career)
   Have you ever **had** an operation? (at any time in your life up to now)
   How many times **has** he **been** married? (in his life)

The adverbs *ever, never,* and *before* are common with this use.
   Have you **ever** been to Australia?
   I've **never** tried bungee jumping.
   I haven't tried sushi **before**.

Questions and answers about definite times are expressed in the Past Simple.
   When **did** you **go** to the United States?
   Was her poetry **published** while she was alive?
   I **broke** my leg once, but I **didn't** have to stay in the hospital.
   He **met** his second wife in the dry cleaner's.

3. a past action that has a present result. The action is usually in the recent past.
   The taxi **hasn't arrived** yet. (We're still waiting for it.)
   What **have** you **done** to your lip? (It's bleeding.)

We often announce news in the Present Perfect because the speaker is emphasizing the event as a present fact.
   Have you **heard**? The prime minister **has resigned**.
   Susan**'s had** her baby!
   I**'ve ruined** the meal.

Details about definite time will be in the Past Simple.
   She **resigned** because she lost a vote of no confidence.
   She **had** a baby boy this morning. It **was** a difficult birth.
   I **didn't watch** it carefully enough.

The adverbs *yet, already,* and *just* are common with this use.
   I haven't done my homework **yet**. (Negative)
   Has the mail come **yet**? (Question)
   I've **already** done my homework.
   She's **just** had some good news.

Final Note
Be careful with *been* and *gone*.
   He's **been** to the United States. (= experience—he isn't there now.)
   She's **gone** to the United States. (= present result—she's there now.)

7.2 Present Perfect or Past Simple?

1. The Present Perfect is for unfinished actions. The Past Simple is for completed actions. Compare:

Present Perfect	**Past Simple**
I've lived in Texas for six years. (I still live there.)	I lived in Texas for six years. (Now I live somewhere else.)
I've written several books. (I can still write some more.)	Shakespeare wrote 30 plays. (He can't write any more.)

2. We can see that the Present Perfect refers to indefinite time and the Past Simple refers to definite time by looking at the time expressions used with the different tenses.

Present Perfect—indefinite		Past Simple—definite	
I've done it	for a long time. since July. before. recently.	I did it	yesterday. last week. two days ago. at 8:00. in 1987. when I was young. for a long time.
I've already done it. I haven't done it yet.			

Be careful with *this morning/afternoon,* etc.

Have you **seen** Amy this morning? (It's still morning.)

Did you **see** Amy this morning? (It's the afternoon or evening.)

7.3 Present Perfect Simple passive

Form

has/have been + past participle (*-ed,* etc.)

It	has been	sold.
They	have been	

Use

The uses are the same in the passive as in the active.
Two million cars **have been produced** so far this year. (unfinished past)
Has she ever **been fired**? (past experience)
"Have you heard? Two hundred homes **have been washed** away by a tidal wave!" (present importance)

7.4 Phrasal verbs

There are four types of phrasal verbs.

Type 1
Verb + particle (no object)
a. He put on his coat and **went out.**
b. I didn't put enough wood on the fire and it **went out.**
In a, the verb and particle are used literally. In b, they are used idiomatically. *To go out* means to stop burning.
Examples with literal meaning:
Sit down.
She **stood up** and **walked out.**
Please **go away.**
She **walked** right **past** the store without noticing it.
Examples with idiomatic meaning:
The marriage didn't **work out.** (= succeed)
Our plans **fell through.** (= fail)

Type 2
Verb + particle + object (separable)
a. I **put up** the picture.
b. I **put up** my sister for the night.
In a, the verb and particle are used literally. In b, they are used idiomatically. *To put up* means to give someone food and a place to sleep usually for the night or a few days.
Type 2 phrasal verbs are separable. The object (noun or pronoun) can come between the verb and the particle.
I **put up** the picture.   I **put up** my sister.
I **put** the picture **up.**   I **put** my sister **up.**

But if the object is a pronoun, it always comes between the verb and the particle.
I put **it** up.   NOT ~~I put up it.~~
I put **her** up.   NOT ~~I put up her.~~
Examples with a literal meaning:
The waiter **took away** the plates.
Don't **throw** it **away.**
They're **tearing** that old building **down.**
Examples with an idiomatic meaning:
I **put off** the meeting. (= postpone)
Don't **let** me **down.** (= disappoint)

Type 3
Verb + particle + object (inseparable)
a. She **came across** the room.
b. She **came across** an old friend while she was out shopping.
In a, the verb and particle are used literally. In b, they are used idiomatically. *To come across* means to find by accident.
Type 3 phrasal verbs are inseparable. The object (noun or pronoun) always comes after the particle.
NOT ~~She came an old friend across.~~ or ~~She came her across.~~
Examples with a literal meaning:
I'm **looking for** Jane.
They **ran across** the park.
We **drove past** them.
Examples with an idiomatic meaning:
I'll **look after** it for you. (= care for)
She **takes after** her father. (= resemble in features, build, character, or disposition)
He never **got over** the death of his wife. (= recover from)

Type 4
Verb + particle + particle
I **get along** very well **with** my boss.
I'm **looking forward to** it.
How can you **put up with** that noise?
Type 4 phrasal verbs are nearly always idiomatic. The object cannot change position. It cannot come before the particles or between the particles.
NOT ~~I'm looking forward it to.~~

Unit 8

Introduction to conditionals

There are many different ways of making sentences with *if.* It is important to understand the difference between sentences that express real possibilities and those that express unreal situations.

Real possibilities
If it **rains**, we**'ll** stay home.
(*if* + Present Simple + *will*)
If you**'ve finished** your work, you **can** go home.
(*if* + Present Perfect + modal auxiliary verb)
If you**'re feeling** ill, **go** home and **get** into bed.
(*if* + Present Continuous + imperative)

Unreal situations
You **would understand** me better if you **came** from my country.
(*would* + *if* + Past Simple)
If I **were** rich, I **wouldn't have** any problems.
(*if* + *were* + *would*)
If I **stopped** smoking, I **could run** faster.
(*if* + Past Simple + modal auxiliary verb)

There are several patterns that you need to know to understand the variations. Note that a comma is usual when the *if* clause comes first.

8.1 First conditional

Form

if + Present Simple + *will*

Affirmative

> If I find your wallet, I'll let you know.
> We'll come and see you on Sunday if the weather's good.

Negative

> You won't pass the test if you don't study.
> If you lose your ticket, you won't be able to go.

Question

> What will you do if you don't find a job?
> If there isn't a hotel, where will you stay?

Note that we do not usually use *will* in the *if* clause.
    NOT ~~If you will leave now, you'll catch the train.~~
           ~~If I'll go out tonight, I'll give you a call.~~
If can be replaced by *unless* (= if … not) or *in case* (= because of the possibility …).
> **Unless** I hear from you, I'll come at 8:00.
> I'll take my umbrella **in case** it rains.

Use

1. First conditional sentences express a possible condition and its probable result in the future.

Condition (*if* clause)	Result (result clause)
If I find a sweater in your size,	I'll buy it for you.
If you can do the homework,	give me a call.
If you can find my purse,	I might buy you ice cream.
If you've never been to Wales,	you should try to go there one day.

2. We can use the first conditional to express different functions (all of which express a possible condition and a probable result).
> If you do that again, I'll kill you! (= a threat)
> Careful! If you touch that, you'll burn yourself! (= a warning)
> I'll mail the letter if you like. (= an offer)
> If you lend me $100, I'll love you forever. (= a promise)

8.2 Time clauses

Conjunctions of time (*when, as soon as, before, until, after*) are not usually followed by *will*. We use a present tense even though the time reference is future.
> I'll call you **when** I **get** home.
> **As soon as** dinner **is** ready, I'll give you a call.
> Can I have a word with you **before** I **go**?
> Wait **until** I **come** back.

We can use the Present Perfect if it is important to show that the action in the time clause is finished.
> **When** I've **finished** the book, I'll lend it to you.
> I'll go home **after** I've **done** the shopping.

8.3 Zero Conditional

Zero Conditional sentences refer to "all time," not just the present or future. They express a situation that is always true. *If* means *when* or *whenever*.
> If you spend over $50 at that supermarket, you get a five percent discount.

8.4 Second conditional

Form

if + Past Simple + *would*

Affirmative

> If I won some money, I'd go around the world.
> My father would kill me if he could see me now.

Negative

> I'd give up my job if I didn't like it.
> If I saw a ghost, I wouldn't talk to it.

Question

> What would you do if you saw someone shoplifting?
> If you needed help, who would you ask?

Note that *was* can change to *were* in the condition clause.

If I If he	were rich,	I he	wouldn't have to work.

Use

1. We use the second conditional to express an unreal situation and its probable result. The situation or condition is improbable, impossible, imaginary, or contrary to known facts.
> If I were the president of my country, I'd increase taxes. (But it's not very likely that I will ever be the president.)
> If my mother was still alive, she'd be very proud. (But she's dead.)
> If Ted needed money, I'd lend it to him. (But he doesn't need it.)
2. Other modal verbs are possible in the result clause.
> I **could** buy some new clothes if I had some money.
> If I saved a little every week, I **might** be able to save up for a car.
> If you wanted that job, you'**d have** to apply very soon.
3. *If I were you, I'd* … is used to give advice.
> **If I were you, I'd** apologize to her.
> **I'd** take it easy for a while **if I were you**.

8.5 First or second conditional?

Both conditionals refer to the present and future. The difference is about probability, not time. It is usually clear which conditional to use. First conditional sentences are real and possible; second conditional sentences express situations that will probably never happen.
> If I lose my job, I'll … (My company is doing badly. There is a strong possibility of being fired.)
> If I lost my job, I'd … (I probably won't lose my job. I'm just speculating.)
> If there is a nuclear war, we'll all … (Said by a pessimist.)
> If there was a nuclear war, … (But I don't think it will happen.)

would

Notice the use of *would* in the following sentences:
> She'**d** look better with shorter hair. (= If she cut her hair, she'd look better.)

***would* to express preference**
> I'**d** love a cup of coffee.
> Where **would** you like to sit?
> I'**d** rather have coffee, please.
> I'**d** rather not tell you, if that's all right.
> What **would** you rather do, stay in or go out?

***would* to express a request**
> **Would** you open the door for me?
> **Would** you mind lending me a hand?

Unit 9

Modal verbs 2

Modal verbs can express ability, obligation, permission, and request. They can also express the idea of probability or how certain a situation is. There is an introduction to modal auxiliary verbs on page 141.

9.1 Expressing possibility/probability

1. *Must* and *can't* express the logical conclusion of a situation: *must* = logically probable; *can't* = logically improbable. We don't have all the facts, so we are not absolutely sure, but we are pretty certain.

> He **must** be exhausted. He can't even stand up.
> Sue **can't** have a ten-year-old daughter! Sue's only 24!
> He's in great shape, even though he **must** be at least 60!
> A walk in this weather! You **must** be joking!
> Is there no answer? They **must** be in bed. They **can't** be out this late!

2. *Could* and *may/might* express possibility in the present or future. *May/Might + not* is the negative. *Couldn't* is rare in this use.

> He **might** be lost.
> They **could** move to a different place.
> Dave and Beth aren't at home. They **could** be at the concert, I suppose.
> We **may** go to Greece for our vacation. We haven't decided yet.
> Take your umbrella. It **might** rain later
> I **might** not be able to come tonight. I **might** have to work late.

Note the Continuous Infinitive
Must/could/can't/might + be + -ing make the Continuous form of these modal verbs.

> You must **be joking**!
> Peter must **be working** late.
> She **could have been lying** to you.

9.2 Expressing possibility/probability: the past

The Perfect Infinitive
Must/could/can't/might + have + past participle express degrees of probability in the past.

Past
> He **must have been** exhausted.
> She **can't have told** him about us yet.
> He **might have gotten** lost.
> They **could have moved** to a different place.

9.3 *So do I! Neither do I!*

When we agree or disagree using *So …/Neither … I*, we repeat the auxiliary verbs. If there is no auxiliary, use *do/does/did*. Be careful with sentence stress.

AGREEING		DISAGREEING	
So … I.			
I like ice cream.	So do I.	I don't like Mary.	I do.
I'm wearing jeans.	So am I.	We're going now.	We aren't.
I can swim.	So can I.	I can speak Polish.	I can't.
I went out.	So did I.	I haven't been skiing.	I have.
Neither … I.			
I don't like working.	Neither do I.	I like blue cheese.	I don't.
I can't drive.	Neither can I.	I saw Pat yesterday.	I didn't.
I haven't been to Paris.	Neither have I.	I'm going to have some coffee.	I'm not.

9.4 *too* and *either/neither*

We express that we have the same ideas as somebody else by using *too* and *either/neither*. With *too* we repeat the auxiliary verbs. If there is no auxiliary, use *do/does/did*.

"I like ice cream."	"I do, too." / "Me too."
"I have always studied hard."	"I have, too." / "Me too."
"I don't like working."	"I don't, either." / "Me neither."
"I can't play a musical instrument."	"I can't, either." / "Me neither."

Unit 10

10.1 Present Perfect Continuous

A note about Continuous forms.
Remember, the following ideas are expressed by all Continuous forms:
1. activity in progress.
   > Be quiet! I'm **thinking**.
   > I **was taking** a shower when the phone rang.
   > I've **been working** since 9:00 this morning.
2. temporary activity.
   > We're **staying** with friends until we find our own place to live.
   > We've **been living** with them for six weeks.
3. possibly incomplete activity.
   > I'm **writing** a report. I have to finish it by tomorrow.
   > Who's **been eating** my sandwich?

Form

Affirmative and negative

I We You They	've haven't	been working.
He She It	's hasn't	

Question

How long	have	I you we	been working?
	has	she it	

Use

We use the Present Perfect Continuous to express:
1. an activity that began in the past and is still continuing now.
   > I've **been studying** English for three years.
   > How long **have** you **been working** here?

   Sometimes there is no difference between the Simple and the Continuous.

I've played I've been playing	the piano since I was a boy.

   If the Continuous is possible, English has a preference for using it.
   The Continuous can sometimes express a temporary activity, and the Simple a permanent state.
   > I've **been living** in this house for the past few months. (= temporary)
   > I've **lived** here all my life. (= permanent)

   Remember that stative verbs rarely take the Continuous (see page 138).
   > I've **had** this book for ages.
   > I've always **loved** sunny days.

2. a past activity that has caused a present result.
   > I've **been working** all day. (I'm tired now.)
   > **Have** you **been crying**? (Your eyes are red.)
   > Roger's **been cutting** the grass. (I can smell it.)

   The past activity might be finished or it might not. The context usually makes this clear.
   > Look out the window! It's **been snowing**! (It has stopped snowing now.)
   > I've **been writing** this book for two years. (It still isn't finished.)
   > I'm covered in paint because I've **been decorating** the bathroom. (It might be finished or it might not. We don't know.)

10.2 Present Perfect Simple or Continuous?

1. The Simple expresses a completed action.
   > I've **painted** the kitchen, and now I'm **doing** the bathroom.

   The Continuous expresses an activity over a period and things that happened during the activity.
   > I have paint in my hair because I've **been decorating**.

   Because the Simple expresses a completed action, we use the Simple if the sentence gives a number or quantity. Here, the Continuous isn't possible.
   > I've been reading all day. I've **read** ten chapters.
   > She's been eating ever since she arrived. She's **eaten** ten cookies already.

2. Some verbs don't have the idea of a long time, for example, *find, start, buy, die, lose, break, stop*. These verbs are more usually found in the Simple.
   Some verbs have the idea of a long time, for example, *wait, work, play, try, learn, rain*. These verbs are often found in the Continuous.
   > I've **cut** my finger. (One short action.)
   > I've **been cutting** firewood. (Perhaps over several hours.)

10.3 Time expressions

Here are some time expressions often found with certain tenses.

Past Simple
> I **lived** in Chicago **for six years**.
> I **saw** Jack **two days ago**.
> They **met during the war**.
> She **got** married **while she was in college**.

Present Perfect
> We've **been** married **for ten years**.
> They've **been living** here **since June**.
> She **hasn't been working since their baby was born**.

Future
> We're **going** on vacation **for a few days**.
> The class **ends in 20 minutes**.
> I'll **be** home **in a half an hour**.

Prepositions with dates, months, years, etc.

in	September 1965 the summer the 1920s the 20th century	on	Monday Monday morning August 8th Christmas Day vacation	at	7:00 the end of May the age of ten dinner time

Unit 11

Look at the following question words. Notice that *What*, *Which*, and *Whose* can combine with a noun and *How* can combine with an adjective or an adverb.

What kind of music do you like?
What size shoe do you wear?
What color are your eyes?
Which pen do you want?
Which way is it to the station?
Whose book is this?
How much do you weigh?
How many brothers and sisters do you have?
How many times have you been on a plane?
How much homework do you get every night?
How tall are you?
How often do you go to the movies?
How long does it take you to get to school?

11.1 Indirect questions

1. Indirect questions have the same word order as the affirmative and there is no *do/does/did*.

   | Tom lives | in California.

   I don't know where | Tom lives |.   NOT ~~I don't know where does Tom live.~~

   Here are some more expressions that introduce indirect questions:

I wonder I can't remember I have no idea I'd like to know I'm not sure	how long the trip takes.

   If there is no question word, use *if* or *whether*.
      I don't know **if** I'm coming or not.
      I wonder **whether** it's going to rain.

2. We often make direct questions into indirect questions to make them sound "softer" or more polite.

Direct question	**Indirect question**	
What time do the banks close?	Could you tell me Do you know Do you happen to know Have you any idea Do you remember	what time the banks close?

11.2 Question tags

Form

1. Question tags are very common in spoken English. The most common patterns are:
   affirmative sentence—negative tag
      You**'re** Jenny, **aren't** you?
   negative sentence—affirmative tag
      It **isn't** a very nice day, **is** it?
2. We repeat the auxiliary verb in the tag. If there is no auxiliary, use *do/does/did*.
      You **haven't** been here before, **have** you?
      You **can** speak French, **can't** you?
      We **should** take the dog out, **shouldn't** we?
      She eats meat, **doesn't** she?
      Banks close at four, **don't** they?
      You went to bed late, **didn't** you?

Note
For negative question tags with *I'm* … use *aren't*.
      I**'m** late, **aren't** I?   NOT ~~I'm late, am't I?~~
But,
      I**'m not** late, **am** I?   NOT ~~I'm not late, aren't I?~~
3. Notice the meaning of *Yes* and *No* in answer to question tags.
      "You're coming, aren't you?"   "Yes." (= I **am** coming.)
                                     "No." (= I**'m not** coming.)

Use

We use question tags to keep a conversation going by involving listeners and inviting them to participate.
The meaning of a question tag depends on how you say it. A question tag with rising intonation is like a real question—it is asking for confirmation. It means "I'm not sure, so I'm checking." The speaker thinks he/she knows the answer, but isn't absolutely certain.

   Your name's Abigail, isn't it?

   You're in advertising, aren't you?

   You work in the city, don't you?

A question tag with falling intonation isn't really a question at all—it is a way of making conversation. It means "Talk to me." The speaker expects people to agree with him/her.

   Beautiful day, isn't it?

   It's wonderful weather for swimming, isn't it?

   That was a great concert, wasn't it?

   You haven't been here before, have you?

Note
We can also use question tags with negative sentences to make a polite request for information or help.

   You couldn't lend me your car this evening, could you?

Unit 12

12.1 Reported speech

Reported statements and tense changes
It is usual for the verb in the reported clause to move "one tense back" if:
1. the reporting verb is in the past tense (e.g., *said*, *told*).

   Present ⟶ Past
   Present Perfect ⟶ Past Perfect
   Past ⟶ Past Perfect

   "I**'m going**."   He said he **was going**.
   "She**'s passed** her test."   He told me she **had passed** her test.
   "My father **died** when I was six."   She said her father **had died** when she was six.
2. we are reporting thoughts and feelings.
      I thought she **was** married, but she isn't.
      I didn't know he **was** a teacher. I thought he **worked** in a bank.
      I forgot you **were coming**. Never mind. Come in.
      I hoped you **would** call.

There is no tense change if:
1. the reporting verb is in the present tense (e.g., *says*, *asks*).
   "The train **will be** late."   He says the train **will be** late.
   "I **come** from Spain."   She says she **comes** from Spain.
2. the reported speech is about something that is still true.
   Rain forests **are being destroyed**.
   She told him that rain forests **are being destroyed**.
   "I **hate** soccer."
   I told him I **hate** soccer.

Note
Some modal verbs change.

can ⟶ could
will ⟶ would
may ⟶ might

   "She **can** type well."   He told me she **could** type well.
   "**I'll** help you."   She said she**'d** help me.
   "I **may** come."   She said she **might** come.

Other modal verbs don't change.
   "You **should** go to bed."   He told me I **should** go to bed.
   "It **might** rain."   She said she thought it **might** rain.
Must can stay as *must*, or it can change to *had to*.
   "I **must** go!"   He said he **must/had to** go.

12.2 Reporting verbs

There are many reporting verbs.
We rarely use *say* with an indirect object (i.e., the person spoken to).
   She said she was going.   NOT ~~She said to me she was going.~~
Tell is always used with an indirect object in reported speech.

She told	me the doctor us her husband	the news.

In more formal situations, we can use *that* after the reporting verb.
   He told her (**that**) he would be home late.
   She said (**that**) sales were down from last year.
Many verbs are more descriptive than *say* and *tell*, for example, *explain*, *interrupt*, *demand*, *insist*, *admit*, *complain*, *warn*.

He	explained complained	that he would be home late.
She	admitted	that sales were down that year.

Sometimes we report the idea, rather than the actual words.
   "I'll lend you some money."   He offered to lend me some money.
   "I won't help you."   She refused to help me.

12.3 Reported questions

1. The word order in reported questions is different in reported speech. There is no inversion of subject and auxiliary verb and there is no *do/does/did*. This is similar to indirect questions (see page 150).
   "Why have you come here?"   I asked her why she had come here.
   "What time is it?"   He wants to know what time it is.
   "Where do you live?"   She asked me where I lived.

Note
We do not use a question mark in a reported question.
We do not use *say* in reported questions.
   He said, "How old are you?"   He asked me how old I am.
2. If there is no question word, use *if* or *whether*.

She wants to know	whether if	she should wear a dress.

12.4 Reported commands, requests, etc.

1. For reported commands, requests, offers, and advice we use verb + person + infinitive.
   They **told us to** go away.
   They **asked me to** look after their cat.
   He **urged the teachers to** go back to work.
   She **persuaded me to** have my hair cut.
   I **advised the president to** leave immediately.

   Note
   Say is not possible. Use *ask*, *told*, etc.

2. For negative commands, use *not* before *to*.
   He told me **not to** tell anyone.
   The police warned people **not to** go out.
3. Be careful! *Tell* and *ask* can be used in different ways, but the form changes.
   We use *tell* for reported statements and reported commands.

   Reported statements

He told me that he was going. They told us that they were going abroad. She told them what had been happening.

   Reported commands

He told me to keep still. The police told people to move on. My parents told me to clean up my room.

   We use *ask* for reported commands and reported questions.

   Reported commands

I was asked to attend the interview. He asked me to open my suitcase. She asked me not to leave.

   Reported questions

He asked me what I did for a living. I asked her how much the rent was. She asked me why I had come.

Appendix 1

IRREGULAR VERBS

Base form	Past Simple	Past Participle
be	was/were	been
beat	beat	beaten
become	became	become
begin	began	begun
bend	bent	bent
bite	bit	bitten
blow	blew	blown
break	broke	broken
bring	brought	brought
build	built	built
burst	burst	burst
buy	bought	bought
can	could	been able
catch	caught	caught
choose	chose	chosen
come	came	come
cost	cost	cost
cut	cut	cut
dig	dug	dug
do	did	done
draw	drew	drawn
drink	drank	drunk
drive	drove	driven
eat	ate	eaten
fall	fell	fallen
feed	fed	fed
feel	felt	felt
fight	fought	fought
find	found	found
fit	fit	fit
fly	flew	flown
forget	forgot	forgotten
forgive	forgave	forgiven
freeze	froze	frozen
get	got	gotten
give	gave	given
go	went	gone
grow	grew	grown
hang	hung	hung
have	had	had
hear	heard	heard
hide	hid	hidden
hit	hit	hit
hold	held	held
hurt	hurt	hurt
keep	kept	kept
kneel	knelt	knelt
know	knew	known
lay	laid	laid
lead	led	led
leave	left	left

Base form	Past Simple	Past Participle
lend	lent	lent
let	let	let
lie	lay	lain
light	lighted/lit	lighted/lit
lose	lost	lost
make	made	made
mean	meant	meant
meet	met	met
must	had to	had to
pay	paid	paid
put	put	put
quit	quit	quit
read /rid/	read /rɛd/	read /rɛd/
ride	rode	ridden
ring	rang	rung
rise	rose	risen
run	ran	run
say	said	said
see	saw	seen
sell	sold	sold
send	sent	sent
set	set	set
shake	shook	shaken
shine	shone	shone
shoot	shot	shot
show	showed	shown
shut	shut	shut
sing	sang	sung
sink	sank	sunk
sit	sat	sat
sleep	slept	slept
slide	slid	slid
speak	spoke	spoken
spend	spent	spent
spread	spread	spread
stand	stood	stood
steal	stole	stolen
stick	stuck	stuck
sweep	swept	swept
swim	swam	swum
take	took	taken
teach	taught	taught
tear	tore	torn
tell	told	told
think	thought	thought
throw	threw	thrown
understand	understood	understood
wake	woke	woken
wear	wore	worn
win	won	won
write	wrote	written

Appendix 2

VERB PATTERNS

Verbs + *to* + infinitive only

agree choose dare decide expect forget help hope learn manage need offer promise refuse seem want would like would love would prefer would hate	to do to come to cook

Notes

1. *Help* and *dare* can be used without *to*.
   We **helped clean up** the kitchen.
   They didn't **dare disagree** with him.
2. *Have to* for obligation.
   I **have to wear** a uniform.
3. *Used to* for past habits.
   I **used to smoke**, but I quit last year.

Verbs + *-ing* only

adore enjoy adore hate don't mind finish look forward to	doing swimming cooking

Note

We often use the verb *go* + *-ing* for sports and activities.
   I **go swimming** every day.
   I **go shopping** on weekends.

Verbs + *-ing* or *to* + infinitive
(with little or no change in meaning)

like love prefer hate can't stand begin start continue	doing to do

Verbs + *-ing* or *to* + infinitive
(with a change in meaning)

remember stop try	doing to do

Notes

1. I **remember mailing** the letter.
   (= I have a memory now of a past action: mailing the letter.)
   I **remembered to mail** the letter.
   (= I reminded myself to mail the letter. I didn't forget.)
2. I **stopped drinking** coffee.
   (= I gave up the habit.)
   I **stopped to drink** a coffee.
   (= I stopped doing something else in order to have a cup of coffee.)
3. I **tried to sleep**.
   (= I wanted to sleep, but it was difficult.)
   I **tried counting** sheep and **drinking** a glass of warm milk.
   (= These were possible ways of getting to sleep.)

Verbs + somebody + *to* + infinitive

advise allow ask beg encourage expect help need invite order remind tell want warn (+ *not*) would like	me him them someone	to do to go to come

Note

Help can be used without *to*.
   I **helped** him **do** the dishes.

Verbs + somebody + infinitive (without *to*)

let make help	her us	do

Notes

1. *To* is used with *make* in the passive.
   We were **made to work** hard.
2. *Let* cannot be used in the passive. *Allowed to* is used instead.
   She was **allowed to leave**.

Phonetic Symbols

Consonants			
1	/p/	as in	**pen** /pɛn/
2	/b/	as in	**big** /bɪg/
3	/t/	as in	**tea** /ti/
4	/d/	as in	**do** /du/
5	/k/	as in	**cat** /kæt/
6	/g/	as in	**go** /goʊ/
7	/f/	as in	**five** /faɪv/
8	/v/	as in	**very** /ˈvɛri/
9	/s/	as in	**son** /sʌn/
10	/z/	as in	**zoo** /zu/
11	/l/	as in	**live** /lɪv/
12	/m/	as in	**my** /maɪ/
13	/n/	as in	**nine** /naɪn/
14	/h/	as in	**happy** /hæpi/
15	/r/	as in	**red** /rɛd/
16	/y/	as in	**yes** /yɛs/
17	/w/	as in	**want** /wɑnt/
18	/θ/	as in	**thanks** /θæŋks/
19	/ð/	as in	**the** /ðə/
20	/ʃ/	as in	**she** /ʃi/
21	/ʒ/	as in	**television** /ˈtɛlɪvɪʒn/
22	/tʃ/	as in	**child** /tʃaɪld/
23	/dʒ/	as in	**Japan** /dʒəˈpæn/
24	/ŋ/	as in	**English** /ˈɪŋglɪʃ/

Vowels			
25	/i/	as in	**see** /si/
26	/ɪ/	as in	**his** /hɪz/
27	/ɛ/	as in	**ten** /tɛn/
28	/æ/	as in	**stamp** /stæmp/
29	/ɑ/	as in	**father** /ˈfɑðər/
30	/ɔ/	as in	**saw** /sɔ/
31	/ʊ/	as in	**book** /bʊk/
32	/u/	as in	**you** /yu/
33	/ʌ/	as in	**sun** /sʌn/
34	/ə/	as in	**about** /əˈbaʊt/
35	/eɪ/	as in	**name** /neɪm/
36	/aɪ/	as in	**my** /maɪ/
37	/ɔɪ/	as in	**boy** /bɔɪ/
38	/aʊ/	as in	**how** /haʊ/
39	/oʊ/	as in	**go** /goʊ/
40	/ər/	as in	**bird** /bərd/
41	/ɪr/	as in	**near** /nɪr/
42	/ɛr/	as in	**hair** /hɛr/
43	/ɑr/	as in	**car** /kɑr/
44	/ɔr/	as in	**more** /mɔr/
45	/ʊr/	as in	**tour** /tʊr/